OEDIPUS TYRANNUS

Tragic Heroism and the
Limits of Knowledge

❖

TWAYNE'S MASTERWORK STUDIES

Robert Lecker, General Editor

OEDIPUS TYRANNUS

Tragic Heroism and the
Limits of Knowledge

✥

Charles Segal

TWAYNE PUBLISHERS ◆ NEW YORK

Maxwell Macmillan Canada ◆ Toronto

Maxwell Macmillan International ◆ New York Oxford Singapore Sydney

Twayne's Masterwork Studies No. 108

Copyright 1993 by Twayne Publishers

Twayne Publishers
Macmillan Publishing Company
866 Third Avenue
New York, New York 10022

Maxwell Macmillan Canada, Inc.
1200 Eglinton Avenue East
Suite 200
Don Mills, Ontario M3C 3N1

Library of Congress Cataloging-in-Publication Data
Segal, Charles, 1936–.
Oedipus tyrannus : tragic heroism and the limits of
knowledge / Charles Segal.
p. cm. — (Twayne's masterwork studies ; 108)
Includes bibliographical references and index.
ISBN 0-8057-7979-5 — ISBN 0-8057-8029-7 (pbk.)
1. Sophocles. Oedipus Rex. 2. Oedipus (Greek mythology) in literature.
3. Knowledge, Theory of, in literature. 4. Heroes in literature. 5. Tragedy.
I. Title. II. Series.
PA4413.07S52 1993

882'.01—dc20

92-32279
CIP

10 9 8 7 6 5 4 3 2 1 (alk. paper)

10 9 8 7 6 5 4 3 2 1 (pbk.: alk. paper)

Printed in the United States of America.

Contents

Illustrations

Note on the References
and Acknowledgments

Sophocles' *Oedipus Tyrannus* is known in English as *Oedipus the King* and in Latin as *Oedipus Rex*. As the Greek word *tyrannos* does not correspond exactly to either the English *king* or the Latin *rex*, I have used the Greek title. I refer to quoted passages from *Oedipus Tyrannus* and *Oedipus Coloneus* (*Oedipus at Colonus* in English) by the line numbers of the Greek text, which are standardized in all modern editions. Of the two most widely used translations of *Oedipus Tyrannus*, David Grene's *The Complete Greek Tragedies* (1959–; University of Chicago Press) closely follows the line numbers of the original Greek, printing them in the text margin. Robert Fagles's *Sophocles: The Three Theban Plays* (1984; Penguin) gives the original line numbers at the top of each page (his line numbers in the margin refer to his translation only).

I generally quote from Fagles's or Grene's translations, but to bring out specific nuances in the Greek original I occasionally translate the text myself; in these cases no translator is indicated in the text. I cite the works of other Greek authors according to the numeration of the Oxford Classical Texts, which most English translations indicate. I have used recent and available translations of these works, but here too I have sometimes translated the text myself—in some cases (indicated in the text) slightly modifying existing translations to bring out aspects of the original Greek.

I have profited greatly from the commentaries and the abundant scholarly literature on the play and the Oedipus myth; and even though I do not always agree with them, I am deeply indebted to the scholarly labors of R. D. Dawe, Lowell Edmunds, Richard C. Jebb, Bernard Knox, Richmond Lattimore, Hugh Lloyd-Jones, Karl Reinhardt, Jean-Marc Moret, Jean-Pierre Vernant, and R. P.

Winnington-Ingram, to mention only a few. Limitations of space do not permit me to acknowledge the many places where I have drawn on previous scholarship or to discuss controversies or differences of interpretation. I have concentrated on those aspects of the play that seem to me most meaningful to the nonspecialist, "Greek-less" reader. Hence I have paid more attention to content than to form, to myth and meaning than to style or staging, although I occasionally touch on these aspects of the play as well. I have tried to take a fresh approach to the text and so have sometimes suggested interpretations that I have not found in the existing literature, which does not mean that someone else somewhere in the enormous body of scholarship on this play has not had the same idea. Frederick Ahl's *Sophocles' Oedipus: Evidence and Self-Conviction* (1991) and Jean Bollack's four-volume commentary, *L'Oedipe Roi de Sophocle* (1990), appeared too late for me to use.

❖

In the last section of chapter 7 and in chapter 11 I have drawn on my study "Time, Theater, and Knowledge in the Tragedy of Oedipus," published in *Edipo: Il teatro greco e la cultura Europea*, edited by B. Gentili and R. Pretagostini (Rome: Edizioni dell' Ateneo, 1986), 459–84, which I have thoroughly revised and recast for this volume. I am grateful to the Edizioni dell' Ateneo for permission to reuse some of the material here.

For helpful discussion, I thank Albert Henrichs and Werner Frick. For ever-courteous and efficient help in the production of the book I thank series editor Robert Lecker, editor Mark Zadrozny, and copy editor Julie Hagen. I am grateful to Lenore Parker and Lowell Bowditch for aid in the preparation of the manuscript. My greatest debt is to my wife, Nancy Jones, for her sustaining patience and wise advice.

Sophocles. Lateran Collection, Vatican Museums, Rome. *Photograph courtesy of Alinari/Art Resource, New York City.*

Chronology

All dates are B.C. *and approximate.*

534	First tragic performance at Athens by Thespis at the Festival of Dionysus, under the tyrant Peisistratus.
525	Aeschylus born.
510–507	Expulsion of the tyrant Peisistratus and foundation of Athenian democracy under the leadership of Cleisthenes.
497	Birth of Sophocles, son of Sophillos, a wealthy inhabitant of the Athenian community of Colonus.
494	Pericles born.
490	King Dareius of Persia invades Greece and is repulsed by the Athenians at Marathon, on the eastern coast of Attica.
ca. 480	Euripides born.
480–478	King Xerxes of Persia invades Greece and is defeated by the Athenian fleet at Salamis and by a Greek land army at Plataea. Aeschylus is said to have fought at Salamis and Sophocles to have danced in the boys' chorus celebrating the victory.
477	Athenians found the Delian League, a naval alliance to protect against further aggression by the Persians; it is a precursor of the Athenian naval empire.
472	Aeschylus presents *The Persians*, dramatizing the Athenian victory at Salamis. The young Pericles is the financial sponsor of the performance.

470 or 469	Socrates born.
468	Sophocles wins his first victory at the dramatic competition with *Triptolemus*, defeating Aeschylus.
467	Aeschylus presents trilogy on the House of Laius, including *Laius*, *Oedipus*, *Seven against Thebes*, and the satyr play *Sphinx*. Only *Seven against Thebes* is extant.
461	Cimon, leader of the aristocratic party, is ostracized; democratic party's influence increases under the leadership of Pericles and Ephialtes.
ca. 460	The historian Thucydides is born.
460–450	Sophocles probably presents *Ajax*.
458	Aeschylus presents *Oresteia*.
457–445	Athenian power expands to Boeotia, the Megarid, and Euboea.
456 or 455	Aeschylus dies in exile at Gela, in Sicily.
454	Treasury of Delian League is moved to Athens; the defensive alliance is visibly transformed into Athenian maritime empire.
449	First victory of Euripides at the dramatic competition.
447	Periclean building program begins: a new temple to Athena, the Parthenon, is begun; construction of a monumental entrance to the Acropolis (the Propylaea) will soon follow.
447–445	Defeated in Boeotia, Athens cuts back its land empire and makes a 30-year peace treaty with Sparta.
444	Invited by Pericles, the Sophist Protagoras helps draft laws and constitution for Athenian colony of Thurii in southern Italy, which the historian Herodotus also visits.
443–442	Sophocles serves as *hellenotamias*, supervising the amount of tribute to be assessed to Athens's island subject-allies.
442–441	Sophocles presents *Antigone*.

441–440	Sophocles elected one of 10 generals to serve in suppressing the revolt of the island of Samos. His election is supposed to have been due to the popularity of *Antigone* during the previous year.
440–430	Sophocles probably presents *Trachinian Women.*
438	Gold and ivory statue of Athena by Pheidias set up in the Parthenon. Euripides presents *Alcestis*, his earliest extant play.
431	Peloponnesian War begins. Athens and Sparta are the principals, but all of Greece is eventually involved. Except for a short, uneasy truce in 421–18, the war will continue until 404, with frequent invasions of Attica by the Spartans and resultant crowding of Athenians from the outlying areas of Attica into the city. Euripides presents *Medea.*
430	Great plague breaks out in Athens.
429	Pericles dies in the plague.
429–425	*Oedipus Tyrannus* probably performed.
428	Euripides presents revised version of *Hippolytus.*
428 or 427	Plato born.
427	Aristophanes presents his first comedy at the dramatic competition. The celebrated Sophist and rhetorician Gorgias of Leontini visits and teaches in Athens. Sophocles possibly serves as a general in the Peloponnesian War.
425	Aristophanes presents *Acharnians*, an antiwar play and the earliest of his comedies to be preserved.
423	Aristophanes presents *Clouds*, satirizing Socrates, the Sophists, and scientific speculation.
421	Aristophanes presents *Peace*. Peace of Nicias begins.
421 or 420	Possible date for production of Euripides' *Electra.*
420	Sophocles is chosen to receive the sacred snake of the healing god Asclepius in his home.

419–410   Sophocles presents *Electra*.

416   Athens conquers the island of Melos, killing men of military age and enslaving the rest of the population.

415   Euripides presents *Trojan Women*, a reflection, in part, on the Athenian harshness toward the Melians.

415–413   Athens's expedition to Sicily under Nicias and Alcibiades ends in a serious defeat for Athens at Syracuse, with the loss of many men and ships. Athens never fully recovers.

414   Aristophanes presents *Birds*, a utopian comedy.

414–412   Euripides' *Ion*, *Iphigeneia among the Taurians*, and *Helen* are presented.

413   Spartans seize and fortify Athenian border town of Decelea, giving them a permanent foothold in Athenian territory.

411–409   Euripides presents *Phoenician Women* (*Phoenissae*), a play about the house of Oedipus.

411   Oligarchical coup at Athens; Sophocles chosen as one of the 10 Probouloi or commissioners. The democracy is replaced by a moderate and conservative oligarchy for only a few months and is then restored.

409   Sophocles, about 85 years old, presents *Philoctetes*, which wins first prize at the dramatic festival in Athens.

408   Euripides goes into exile from Athens and takes up residence at the court of King Archelaus in Macedonia.

406   Sophocles dies; receives a hero cult after his death as Dexion (the "Receiver") for having entertained the sacred snake of Asclepius.

405   Euripides dies. Aristophanes presents *Frogs*, reflecting on the status of tragedy after the deaths of the great tragedians.

404–403   Athens surrenders and Sparta establishes a garrison there.

401   Sophocles' grandson presents *Oedipus at Colonus*.

399   Trial and death of Socrates.

LITERARY AND
HISTORICAL CONTEXT

❖

1

Historical and Cultural
Background

Sophocles wrote *Oedipus Tyrannus* during a period of both extraordinary intellectual and artistic energy and crisis. Under its astute and ambitious statesman, Pericles, Athens became the most powerful city-state in Greece, and by 440 B.C. it was the acknowledged leader in almost every area of cultural activity and a center for philosophy, literature, architecture, sculpture, and painting at a level that has rarely been surpassed.

Why such an outburst of creativity in this time and place? One can only guess at some contributing factors: the development of a fairly stable democratic constitution at the very beginning of the century; the confidence gained from defeating the Persian invaders, first on land at Marathon (490), then at sea at Salamis (480); the buildup of a powerful navy, which gradually developed into a maritime empire that exacted tribute from the island and coastal cities of the eastern Aegean in return for protection against Persia; and, finally, the native energy and initiative of the people. Of no small importance was the gifted leadership of Pericles, a man of wealthy and aristocratic origins who early in his career joined the democratic faction and guided Athens toward Hellenic leadership with a grand, if sometimes ruthless, vision of its cultural and political supremacy.

Pericles was and is controversial—cold, aloof, and ambitious but intensely patriotic. He sponsored the elaborate rebuilding of the Acropolis, which had been burned by the invading Persians in 480, with the magnificent new temple of Athena known as the Parthenon, a grandiose entrance known as the Propylaea, and two other smaller temples completed after his death: the complex but graceful Erechtheum, with its famous caryatids, and the exquisite small Ionic temple to Athena Nike (Athena as Victory)—buildings whose beauty, even after the wear of 25 centuries, still astounds and inspires the visitor. Pericles was also the patron of the greatest sculptor of the age, Pheidias, who executed the famous gold and ivory statue of Athena for the Parthenon, and also designed the great frieze that adorns the inner colonnade.

The rebuilding of the Acropolis was only a small part of Pericles' program. He also oversaw the building of the massive temple to Athena and Hephaestus, known as the Hephaesteum, that rises above the Agora, or marketplace; the Odeion, or musical theater, beneath the Acropolis, adjoining the great theater of Dionysus (and the rebuilding of the theater itself); a new hall for the sanctuary of Demeter for the Eleusinian Mysteries just outside Athens; and several other temples in and around the city. He consolidated Athens's military security by building the Long Walls to connect the city with its harbors and thus make Athens as much of an island as its geography would permit. And Athens became a center for the manufacture of the elegantly painted vases in the style known as Attic red-figure, which were exported all over the Mediterranean. The celebrated painter Polygnotus worked at Athens and Delphi; although his work is not extant, we know it through the descriptions of later writers.

In addition to these visible achievements in art and architecture, Pericles brought to Athens the most inquiring minds of his time. He surrounded himself with poets and philosophers, thinkers and historians. Among his friends were Herodotus, whose *History of the Persian Wars* created history writing as we know it, and the Ionian philosopher-scientist Anaxagoras, who speculated that an ethereal substance called Mind (*Nous*) governed the world and that all of life could be explained by physical processes and the interactions of material substances.

Such rationalistic physical speculation, characteristic of Greek philosophy in the sixth and fifth centuries B.C., naturally aroused suspicion among the more conservative Athenians, as it challenged the traditional anthropomorphic divinities of the Greek pantheon. Aristophanes, for example, made popular entertainment out of the novel scientific theories in his comedy the *Clouds* (423), which parodies thinkers like Anaxagoras for dethroning Zeus with a new god, the scientific principle Whirl or Vortex. The suspicion of intellectuals also had more serious results; Pericles' political enemies tried to get at him by charging Anaxagoras with impiety and forcing him to flee Athens, sometime around the outbreak of the Peloponnesian War in 431. Some 30 years later Socrates was put to death on a similar charge, and political motives were probably paramount with his accusers as well.

Such attacks on freedom of thought, however, were rare. Athens under Pericles was a place where many diverse currents of thought could mingle and conflict, as one can see in the comedies of Aristophanes, such as *Clouds* or *Birds*. The comic poets lampooned the city's leaders (Pericles included) with an exuberant license that was only occasionally checked. Athens's wealth and intellectualism drew the traveling teachers and thinkers known as the Sophists, who speculated and lectured (for pay) on a wide range of controversial subjects: religion, the origins of law and society, political and domestic management, and the language skills that assured success in the public assemblies and law courts.

Visiting Athens in 427, the Sicilian rhetorician and philosopher Gorgias made a sensation by displaying his intricate style of oratory and argumentation. A few years later the visit of another celebrated Sophist, Protagoras, provided the setting for Plato's dialogue of that name, *Protagoras*, which concerned the Sophist's claim to be able to teach civic skill or political virtue as a practical art or technique.

Protagoras was the best known of the Sophists, and his example is instructive. He ranged widely over many controversial areas, and, like his fellow intellectuals, he emphasized the power of human reason to confront and resolve the mysteries of existence. Among his sayings, two are particularly famous: "Of all things man [or, a man] is the measure, of the things that are, that they are, and of the things that are not, that they are not"; and "Concerning the gods I have no means of knowledge, either that they exist or that they do not exist; for many are the things that hinder knowing, the obscurity [of the subject] and the brevity of human life." Despite the uncertainties about these sayings' contexts and some details of their interpretation, both express the human-centered, rationalistic speculation that is embodied to some extent in the hero of *Oedipus*.

Besides its artistic merits, then, *Oedipus* is a major document in one of the most far-reaching intellectual revolutions in Western history, sometimes known as the Fifth-Century Enlightenment.[1] This period is marked by a shift from the mythical and symbolic thinking characteristic of archaic poets—like Homer, Hesiod, and Pindar—to more conceptual and abstract modes of thought, according to which the world operated through nonpersonal processes that followed predictable scientific laws. Instead of being regarded as an all-giving mother, for example, the earth is conceived of as a measurable surface that men could mine and plow in their mastery of the world. The sun was not a god driving a blazing chariot across the heavens but—as Anaxagoras taught—a huge molten rock, about the size of the Peloponnesus. The gods might be regarded as psychological forces within man—as Euripides suggests for Aphrodite in *Hippolytus*—or as allegorical expressions of the forces of nature. Religion itself was a human invention, a useful means of control in man's gradual creation of the social order necessary for his survival. Laws were not necessarily given by the gods; they were the creations of human assemblies and councils. Cities were not the seat of divine powers rooted in a sacred landscape but human institutions, planned and placed by men in the environments best suited for human habitation. Disease was not the visitation of divine punishment or the manifestation of a pollution or a family curse but the result of an imbalance in the physical organism. As Hippocrates wrote at the opening of his treatise *On the Sacred Disease*, "In no way does this disease [probably epilepsy] seem to me more divine than other diseases or more sacred, but it has a physical basis and cause; out of inexperience and wonderment that it is unlike other diseases, men have supposed it to be a divine matter."

This new confidence in man's power to understand and shape his world found visual expression in sculpture and painting and especially in a new exaltation of the human body—particularly the nude male body—as the ideal of beauty. In these works the human form often appears in movement or energetic action, but with a remarkable formal symmetry and equipoise that suggest dignity, calm, and confident control even in the most strenuous exertions. This style, known as classical, is best represented by the sculptures of Pheidias and Polyclitus. (From Argos, Polyclitus was one of the few major non-Athenian artists of the period. Most of his work survives only in Roman copies.) The frieze of the Parthenon, designed and partly executed by Pheidias, is probably the greatest surviving masterpiece of the period. Depicting the citizens of Athens and their gods in a religious procession, it is the fullest realization of that mixture of harmony, energy, grandeur, simplicity, and idealized human beauty that constitutes the classical style.

The fullest literary expression of this humanistic confidence is the famous first stasimon, or choral ode, of Sophocles' *Antigone*, which begins "Many the wonders but nothing walks stranger than man. / This thing crosses the sea in the winter's storm, / making his path through the roaring waves . . ." (Grene, 332–35). The ode goes on to celebrate man's domination of earth and its creatures, and his discovery of the arts of sailing, politics, and medicine. In fact, this Ode on Man, as it is often called, only scratches the surface of the Periclean achievement, which laid the foundation for Western conceptions of astronomy, mathematics, physics, city planning, architecture, musical theory, science, philosophy, politics, and history.

Philosophers roughly contemporary with Sophocles, like Parmenides of Elea and Empedocles of Acragas, speculated about perception and the relation among the senses in constructing reality. Parmenides in particular made a radical division between Being and Non-Being: with Being belonged light and truth; with Non-Being, night, darkness, opinion, and error. The deceptiveness of the senses and the concealment of ultimate reality beneath false appearances are dominant themes throughout the period in both philosophy and literature. In *Oedipus* Sophocles shares this concern with finding truth in a world of appearances and is influenced, even if indirectly, by the new theories about language: the problem of the relation of words to reality, and the power of words to deceive, to win unjust causes, and to confuse moral issues.

Interest in the potential ambiguity of language parallels interest in the deceptiveness of appearances. In Euripides' *Hippolytus* of

428 B.C.—a play that is, in a way, *Oedipus* in reverse—the hero is falsely accused of incest with his stepmother and is killed by the curse of his enraged father, Theseus, who complains bitterly, "Alas, mortals should have clear evidence to show who are their friends, and also a means of distinguishing their hearts, to see who is truly friend and who is not. And all men should have two voices, one of justice and one as it happens to be, so that the voice of unjust thoughts would be tested and refuted by the just voice, and so we would not be deceived" (925–31).

Skeptical and rationalistic explanations of oracles, of the nature of the gods, and of the origin of religion find echoes in the historians Herodotus and Thucydides and in Sophocles' younger contemporary, Euripides. To take one example, Hecuba in Euripides' *Trojan Women* wonders whether Zeus may be the "necessity of nature or the mind of mortals" (ll. 884–85). Euripides is here drawing on a philosophical view of the gods as impersonal governing forces (nature's necessity) rather than anthropomorphic beings.

In a society as deeply traditional as that of ancient Greece, old ways of thinking often persisted alongside the new. Thus Greek tragedy, and particularly Sophoclean tragedy, is a kind of dialogue between the older and newer ways of looking at the world. Indeed, much of the creative energy in Periclean art and literature derives from this transition between different conceptions of reality. *Antigone* and *Oedipus* raise questions about the power of human reason and suggest that man's life is still surrounded by the mysterious forces of the archaic worldview—forces less amenable to human understanding. According to the older paradigm, nature is not merely an inert, passive object for human domination; it is an organically connected network of animate beings that stand in delicately balanced, mutually responsive relation to one another. Imbalance or violation in one area will produce some kind of disturbance in another, and the resultant disaster and its ramifications may be on a far greater scale than the original crime. Such is the case with the plague that sets the tragic action of *Oedipus Tyrannus* into motion.

THE PLAGUE, THE WAR, AND THE TRAGEDY OF ATHENS

Among the unforeseen catastrophes of the Peloponnesian War that broke out between Athens and Sparta in 431 was the great plague that ravaged Athens between 429 and 425. It spread quickly among both country and city people, who were crammed together behind the walls of Athens when the Spartans invaded, and it destroyed a quarter of the population. The victims included Pericles in 429—a loss that the city was to feel keenly, as men of lesser intelligence and foresight succeeded him. *Oedipus Tyrannus* is almost certainly a response to events of this period. An unexpected, supernatural-seeming disaster suddenly sweeps away brilliant hopes; confidence in human reason and calculation is shattered, and greatness swiftly turns into misery.

Thucydides, the Athenian general and historian who lived through the war and the plague, attributes to Pericles a brilliant speech that sets forth that leader's idealized vision of Athens (*The Peloponnesian War*, 2.35–46). Known as Pericles' Funeral Oration because its occasion is the commemoration of the soldiers who died in the first year of the war, the speech is an encomium to Athens, a "hymn" to the city, as Pericles calls it (*The Peloponnesian War*, 2.41–42). He contrasts Athens's free inquiry, individual initiative, democratic openness, cultural vitality, and diversity to Sparta's closed, suspicious militarism. "Love of the beautiful with a spare toughness, love of intellectual pursuits without softness" is his famous phrase for his beloved city's spirit (*The Peloponnesian War*, 2.40). In its energy in war and peace, its festivals open to everyone (and Pericles is surely thinking of the dramatic festivals too), its welcoming of leading intellectuals from all over, and its democratic institutions, Athens is "the education of Greece" (*The Peloponnesian War*, 2.41).

Having achieved so much, says Pericles, the Athenians have more at stake than others in the war, for they have more to lose. Yet lose they did, although only after more than 20 years of fighting. By the end of the next year, 429, the great plague broke out, and Pericles was dead. "In name it was a democracy," Thucydides says, summing up Pericles' years of power, "but in fact it was rule under the first man" (*The Peloponnesian War*, 2.65). By juxtaposing Pericles' idealized Athens in the Funeral Oration with the fearful

9

moral and psychological disintegration brought by the plague (*The Peloponnesian War*, 2.53), Thucydides himself imposes a tragic structure on the events, a reversal from high to low. It would be surprising if other contemporaries—like Sophocles—did not also see a tragic pattern.

The breakdown of law and of respect for the gods that Thucydides describes as taking place during the plague may find resonances in the second stasimon of *Oedipus*, where the chorus complains of declining reverence for the gods (883–910). The crises and anxieties of the war, Thucydides reports in *The Peloponnesian War*, bring an increasing interest in oracles, and this atmosphere too may have contributed to *Oedipus*'s concerns. The mixture of helplessness, desperation, superstition, and religiosity that followed on the outbreak of the plague (*The Peloponnesian War*, 2.47) is not far from the atmosphere that Sophocles creates in Thebes in the opening scenes of *Oedipus*.

Another circumstance connects Pericles and Oedipus. Pericles' ancient and powerful family, the Alcmaeonids, had been under an old curse for blood pollution, and one of Sparta's opening moves in the war was to demand that the Athenians drive out the accursed clan—a ploy that only endeared Pericles all the more to his fellow citizens.

Sophocles was a close friend of Pericles and held important posts during the leader's ascendancy. But Sophocles' more conservative religious spirit may well have made him uneasy about his friend's freethinking intellectualism and his association with philosopher-scientists like Anaxagoras. It would be an oversimplification to read *Oedipus* as a religious critique of Pericles' humanism, or even as an expression of anxiety about his approximation to the power of a "tyrant."[2] Yet Sophocles' conception of Oedipus probably owes something to the life of Pericles, a man famous for the dispassionate rationalism that won him the nickname "the Olympian."

Pericles' death from the plague may have inspired the theme of Oedipus's fall. Events beyond human control thwart a leader's victory for his city, as with Pericles' careful planning for Athens's victory over its enemy, Sparta, in the Peloponnesian War and Oedipus's salvation of Thebes with his victory over the Sphinx. The play could, then, have been seen by Sophocles' contemporaries as not just a warning against pride or confidence but a compassionate recognition that a great man's noble enterprise can collapse because of unforeseen events—or simply as an objective statement of life's uncertainties, of which Pericles was the most striking recent instance.

As Bernard Knox has brilliantly argued, the figure of Oedipus may also be a distillation of Athens at the height of its power, energy, daring, intellectual curiosity, and confidence in human reason.[3] Athens, rather than Pericles, is the "tyrant," holding its maritime empire with an iron fist when necessary, as it did during repeated attempts by the subject "allies" to revolt. In the last of the three speeches that Thucydides attributes to Pericles, the Athenian leader warns that Athens holds its sea empire as a "tyranny," the surrender of which "is as dangerous as its possession, in the eyes of many, is unjust" (*The Peloponnesian War*, 2.63). Thus the title *Oedipus Tyrannus*, as Knox suggests, may be due to this recognition of the potential tragedy of the "tyrant" city.

We may never know for certain the full extent of *Oedipus*'s relation to contemporary events. It is even possible that Oedipus's search for who he really is reflects something of a communal identity crisis in a city that had undergone a massive transformation in a short time and had refashioned itself from a rather quiet, traditional aristocracy and tyranny in the sixth century into a radical, intellectualized democracy and a powerful empire.[4] Given the intensely political nature of life in Athens and in its dramatic competitions, some connection with politics is highly probable. Like every great work of art, however, the play transcends its immediate historical context. It is one of the great meditations on the mystery of our place in a world that, despite our enormous power and intelligence, we can only partially control and understand.

2

Why Read *Oedipus Tyrannus*?

The place of the *Oedipus Tyrannus* in literature is something like that of the Mona Lisa in art. Everyone knows the story, the first detective story of Western literature; everyone who has read or seen it is drawn into its enigmas and moral dilemmas. It presents a kind of nightmare vision of a world suddenly turned upside down: a decent man discovers that he has unknowingly killed his father, married his mother, and sired children by her. It is a story that, as Aristotle says in the *Poetics*, makes one shudder with horror and feel pity just on hearing it (1453b5). In Sophocles' hands, however, this ancient tale becomes a profound meditation on the questions of guilt and responsibility, the order (or disorder) of our world, and the nature of man. The play stands with the Book of Job, *Hamlet*, and *King Lear* as one of Western literature's most searching examinations of the problem of suffering.

A life that seems happy, productive, and in the service of others suddenly crumbles into dust. The well-meaning king of Thebes—an effective, admired, and respected ruler—suddenly finds that he is not only the source of the calamity from which he has tried to protect his citizens—the plague with which the play begins—but also guilty of the two most horrible crimes imaginable: incest with his mother and the bloody killing of his father. The hero's determined march toward the horrifying discovery of these facts produces the feeling of an inexorable doom surrounding his life, as he recognizes that he has fulfilled prophecies that Apollo had given to him and his parents. In fact, the attempts to avoid these prophecies seem to have brought them to pass. Thus, on one reading, the play is a tragedy about a destiny that the hero cannot evade, despite his best attempts to do so.

The play is a tragedy not only of destiny but also of personal identity: the search for the origins and meaning of our life, our balance between one and many selves, our recognition of the large areas of darkness about who we really are, and the effort to explore the essential mystery of our selfhood. It dramatizes the lonely path of self-discovery, as Oedipus separates his true self from an illusory self defined by the external status of his kingship, and retraces his existence from powerful ruler to lonely wanderer without parents, city, home, or even a sure name. The hero chosen to perform exceptional deeds has also to undergo exceptional suffering as the polluted parricide and outcast who has infected his city.

Oedipus's story serves as the myth not only of Western personal identity but also of Western cultural identity. In this role he may be paired with the figure of Prometheus in Aeschylus's *Prometheus Bound.* Knowledge in *Oedipus Tyrannus* is the reverse of that in Aeschylus's play, where Prometheus's gift to man is allowing man not to foresee the day of his doom. Prometheus keeps technological man away from knowing his death and thus from contemplating the ultimate meaning of his life. To develop the arts and sciences necessary for the basic needs of society, introspective concerns with identity and ultimate meanings are an obstacle, and a certain degree of metaphysical blindness is an advantage. Hence Prometheus's gift that we not know the day of our death.

Prometheus places us close to the origins of the world; it takes us to beginnings still marked by man's primordial struggle with nature for survival. *Oedipus* describes the tragedy of humanity at a later stage, when a reflective awareness of the world within becomes more important than domination of the world outside. This post-Promethean knowledge is tragic rather than technological; it is a knowledge that looks to ends and ultimate reality rather than to means and immediate goals. Its hero has the fearful task, full of suffering, of unveiling the potential chaos of his world.

At the end of his life, in *Oedipus at Colonus,* Sophocles returns to Oedipus, whom he again characterizes as a paradoxical combination of knowledge, power, and weakness. Now in extreme old age, Oedipus appears as the wandering, defenseless exile from Thebes, a blind and homeless beggar. But he is also the vehicle of mysterious blessings that he will bring to Athens, the city in which he is to be buried and that he will henceforth defend through the magical power of his bones.

Freud saw *Oedipus Tyrannus* as a story of a man's deepest and most hidden sexual and aggressive impulses and made it the founding myth of psychoanalysis (see Chapter 5). For the general reader today, Oedipus's situation touches another area of anxiety, existential rather than sexual or psychological: the fear of meaninglessness. Oedipus confronts the mystery of being alive in a world that does not correspond to a pattern of order or justice satisfactory to the human mind. He places us in a tragic universe where we have to ask whether the horrible suffering we witness is all due to design or to chance, whether our lives are random or entirely determined. If everything is by accident—a view to which the modern reader is probably more inclined than the ancient one—then life seems absurd. If it is all by design, then the gods seem cruel or unjust, and life is hell. Sophocles does not give a final answer, any more than Shakespeare offers us a final answer for the tragic shape of Hamlet's life or for the death of Cordelia in *King Lear*.

If *Oedipus Tyrannus* is the quintessential tragedy because of its content, it is also the quintessentially classic work in its form. It embodies the "classic" in its combination of intensely powerful emotions contained in an austere, controlled structure. Both plot structure and language operate within a severe economy that is both dense and lucid. The rhythm of Oedipus's search and discovery has no equal in theater. The bits of information come naturally, randomly, and yet inevitably, and we watch with horror as Oedipus is forced to the terrible conclusion. Every detail, virtually every sentence, contributes to the dramatic effect, and nothing seems superfluous. The language is powerful in its immediate context but often carries a double or triple meaning.

Sophocles' play asks, Why do our lives turn out to have the shape that they finally have? He opens before us a kaleidoscopic configuration of different possibilities: the circumstances of our birth, our character, parental nurture or its absence, sheer luck, a mistake or miscalculation or wrong decision at a crucial moment, a mysterious doom or destiny, will of the gods. Over the centuries readers and audiences have found different answers and emphasized different aspects of the play. There is so much in Sophocles' dense weaving of the simple and the complex that, as the classicist and translator Richmond Lattimore wrote, "We can read *Oedipus* as many times as we like, and every time find new truths and throw away old falsehoods that once seemed to be true. There is always a dimension that escapes."[1]

3

Reception and Influence

Oedipus Tyrannus did not win the first prize when Sophocles presented it in the 420s B.C.; it lost to an unknown play by an obscure tragedian named Philocles.[1] History, however, has reversed the judgment of the Athenians and compensated Sophocles with a posthumous victory beyond his wildest dreams. Since antiquity *Oedipus* has been the most famous play of Greek drama, and it has remained in the consciousness of the West almost continuously for the past 24 centuries. The young Julius Caesar wrote an *Oedipus*, and the Emperor Nero acted in one.[2] Since Aristotle's *Poetics* (around 340–20 B.C.) the play has entered into almost every major discussion of the nature of tragedy, and since Freud's *Interpretation of Dreams* (1900) it has entered into almost every major discussion of psychology, as indeed it still does (see Chapter 5).

Oedipus and six other of Sophocles' plays (out of some 120 that he wrote) have survived because the scholars of late antiquity and Byzantium chose them for teaching in the schools—their way of creating a canon of "great books." Our oldest manuscript, now in the Laurentian Library in Florence, dates from around A.D. 950; some 200 other manuscripts of *Oedipus*, of varying value, are extant, dating from the thirteenth to the fifteenth century. This is an indication of the play's immense prestige in the Byzantine world.

We have only limited knowledge of how the play was transmitted from Sophocles' time to the surviving medieval manuscripts. We may assume that copies of the play, probably in very limited numbers, circulated in the form of papyrus rolls in Sophocles' day. Such rolls have almost entirely perished in Greece, but since the begin-

16

ning of the twentieth century fragments—and, very rarely, entire rolls—have been discovered in Egypt, whose dry climate has preserved them. Most of these papyrus fragments are from the second century A.D. and later. Small portions of Sophocles' lost plays have been recovered in this way, but so far these discoveries have not significantly changed the text of *Oedipus*.

An official copy of the texts of the tragedians was made for the state archives of Athens late in the fourth century B.C. This probably formed the basis for the texts edited by the scholars of the Hellenistic world, principally at Alexandria in Ptolemaic Egypt, from the third century B.C. on. These texts were then copied into parchment books in the third and fourth centuries A.D. Beginning some 600 years later, in the Byzantine empire of Greece and Asia Minor, they were in turn copied into the parchment manuscripts that we have, and from these Byzantine manuscripts come our modern texts of Sophocles.

Unfortunately, this long process of transmission has introduced numerous errors into the texts, partly because the forms of Greek script changed over the centuries and partly because the ancient and poetic language was often misunderstood or miscopied by scribes. Correcting these errors in order to get closer to what Sophocles actually wrote has been the work of classical philologists over the last 400 years, and the process continues. Although the Greek text of *Oedipus* is basically sound, a few corrupt passages remain, and in these cases translators and interpreters have to rely on the conjectures of modern scholars.

THE MIDDLE AGES

Because Greek was little known in Western Europe during most of the Middle Ages, *Oedipus Tyrannus* (or, properly speaking, the myth of Oedipus) was known primarily through Latin authors. During the Middle Ages Statius's long epic poem in Latin, the *Thebaid* (written around A.D. 90), was one of the main vehicles for the influence of *Oedipus Tyrannus*. The poem opens with a long speech by the shade of Oedipus in Hades telling his story and cursing his sons for neglecting him (*Thebaid*, 1.46–87). This work, possibly through a medieval Latin adaptation, lies behind the long twelfth-century epic poem, the *Roman de Thèbes*. It transforms into the terms of knightly chivalry the struggle between Oedipus's two sons, Polyneices and Eteocles, for the throne of Thebes. The *Roman de Thèbes* expands Statius's prologue into some 900 lines, adding some characteristically courtly touches: the drunken Corinthian who taunts Oedipus with bastardy is replaced by a group of jealous courtiers; Oedipus not only solves the riddle of the Sphinx but also kills it and cuts it into pieces; Queen Jocasta is not merely given to Oedipus as his reward but falls in love with him, in the courtly manner, when she sees him at the celebratory banquet. On the other hand, drawing on a detail in Statius's *Thebaid* (itself perhaps influenced by Seneca), the *Roman de Thèbes* gives a particularly lurid account of the self-blinding. The sons find the torn out eye-balls on the ground and, in their horror at the incest, trample on them. Oedipus later undertakes a voluntary penance for his deeds and has himself imprisoned—a Christianized version of the legend that survives in the Oedipus-like story about Pope Gregory the Great (see Chapter 5).

Statius's poem probably also lies behind the account of Jocasta's sufferings in Boccaccio's *De Claris Mulieribus* (*On Famous Women*, 1361–62), from which Christine de Pizan borrows for her *Book of the City of Ladies* (1405) in France and Hans Sachs borrows for his *The Unfortunate Queen Jocasta* (1550) in Germany. Pictorial depictions of the story of Oedipus also exist in several late medieval manuscripts. Particularly striking is the pathetic representation of the exposed baby, hung naked and upside down by his pierced ankles in a tree. In a thirteenth-century manuscript Oedipus kills the Sphinx not by answering the riddle but by striking it through the neck with a huge sword.[3]

THE RENAISSANCE

At the beginning of the fifteenth century, as part of the great revival of interest in classical culture known as the Renaissance, Italian scholars began acquiring Greek manuscripts from the Byzantine world. By the beginning of the century, there were four known

Sophocles manuscripts in Italy, the earliest bought by Niccolò
Niccoli in 1417; by the end of the century there were more than
30.[4] The first Sophocles text to be published in Western Europe
was printed (in Greek) in 1502 by the Venetian publisher Aldus
Manutius (Aldo Manuzio). Translations into Italian began in the
second half of the sixteenth century, and at least four were made
between about 1560 and 1600.

In 1580 the French dramatist Robert Garnier wrote an
Antigone whose first half draws heavily on *Oedipus* but strongly
emphasizes Oedipus's sense of his predestination and damna-
tion—themes of great importance in the religious thought of the
time. Despite the West's steadily increasing knowledge of Greek and
familiarity with Sophocles' plays, however, Seneca's more violent
and sensational version of *Oedipus Tyrannus*—with its melodrama,
necromancy, and ghosts—remained popular and, as we shall see,
often entered into later adaptations of *Oedipus*.

On 3 March 1585 *Oedipus Tyrannus* made its formal debut in
a Western theater. The occasion was the opening of the grand neo-
classic Teatro Olimpico (Olympic Theater), designed by the
sixteenth-century architect Palladio in the northern Italian city of
Vicenza under the sponsorship of the city's Olympian Academy. The
play was translated into Italian by Orsatto Giustiniani, with choruses set to music by Angelo Gabrieli. *Oedipus* was chosen because
it was felt to be the most eminent dramatic work of classical antiquity, in an age that passionately hoped to re-create and emulate the
lost grandeur of the classical world. The theater's elegant interior,
however, was in fact more the enclosed Roman theater than the
simple open-air Greek one, and the audience of select nobles and
literati was far from the citizen audience that would have attended
the original performance. Still, *Oedipus Tyrannus* was launched on
its new career and entered the mainstream of modern Western
literature.

ARISTOTLE'S *POETICS* AND OTHER ANCIENT CRITICISM

We must here retrace our steps and follow the celebrity of *Oedipus*
back to its source in Aristotle, for whom Oedipus was the tragic

hero par excellence. Aristotle considered him the protagonist best suited to tragic action because he represents a man "in great repute and good fortune," "not exceptional for excellence and justice, who undergoes a change to misfortune not on account of baseness or villainy but on account of some error" (*Poetics*, 13.1453a8ff). The word *hamartia*, translated as "error" here, has long been the subject of intense controversy; it is now generally agreed to mean "intellectual mistake," not moral error or "flaw" of character.

The power of *Oedipus*, according to Aristotle, lies in its characteristic tragic effect of arousing and "cleansing" (or purifying) pity and fear (what Aristotle called catharsis); this is produced by action involving family members or loved ones. It is essential for the tragedy, as Aristotle recognizes, that Oedipus has committed his crimes in ignorance. Though stained by the pollutions of these acts, he is both guilty and innocent.

To Aristotle, *Oedipus* also exemplifies the best type of tragic plot. The events are not illogical or unlikely, except perhaps in the case of necessary background material that lies outside the play itself, such as Oedipus's not knowing how Laius was killed (*Poetics*, 24.1460a27–31). Aristotle admired the plausibility of the reversal (peripety, or *peripeteia*) and the dramatic irony in that the Messenger who comes to free Oedipus from his fears has exactly the opposite effect (*Poetics*, 10.1452a24). The recognition of the truth (*anagnorisis*) in *Oedipus*, Aristotle says, is the finest in tragedy because it coincides with the reversal in Oedipus's fortunes (*Poetics*, 11.1452a32). Aristotle does not explain why this should be so, but he may have thought that the tragic effect of pity and fear was enhanced when the audience experiences simultaneously the intellectual process of the recognition and the emotional pathos of the reversal.

Later critics followed Aristotle's judgment. Longinus, author of the interesting treatise *On the Sublime* (probably late first century A.D.), remarks that *Oedipus* alone is worth the entire production of Sophocles' rival, Ion of Chios. Elsewhere Longinus praises the power of Oedipus's cry of horror at his incestuous marriage. He also praises the finale of *Oedipus at Colonus* for its vivid presentation of Oedipus's mysterious call from the gods (*On the Sublime*, 33.5, 23.3, and 15.7, respectively).

SENECA'S OEDIPUS

The Stoic philosopher and tutor of Nero, Lucius Annaeus Seneca (ca. 4 B.C. to A.D. 65), composed 10 tragedies, two of which deal with Oedipus. Seneca's Oedipus influenced many of the later adaptations of the story: it reduces the chorus's role and curtails both the civic ritual and the public/political setting, all of which had little meaning after the demise of the independent Greek city-state and the weakening of the Olympian religion. Like many of the later adapters, Seneca also shifts the emphasis from the hero's intellectual quest to an atmosphere of terror and helplessness.

Like Sophocles, Seneca opens his Oedipus with the plague, but the mood is far more introspective and psychological. Indeed, the plague is more convincing as a symbolic meditation on the infectious nature of evil in the world than as a pollution arising from the hidden stain of blood. Instead of confronting the citizens of Thebes in a public scene and with bold confidence, Seneca's Oedipus speaks a long, dark monologue full of foreboding and a brooding sense of guilt. The truth is revealed through a long account by Laius's ghost, with an accompanying atmosphere of evil omens, heavy shadows, chill swamps, bloody altars, horrid entrails, and the like (Oedipus, 530–658). Covered with blood from his wounds, the dead Laius arises as an avenging spirit from Hades. He is the objectification of the guilt that Oedipus expressed in the prologue, and he utters terrible accusations and threats against his parricidal son.

The recognition in Seneca's play follows Sophocles, but with some major changes. Oedipus's accusation of Creon provides the occasion for an exchange of cynical epigrams, in Seneca's best manner, on the necessity for fear and hatred in holding royal power (Oedipus, 699–706). The self-blinding is motivated by guilt rather than the Sophoclean motifs of religious feeling, the self-pronounced curse, and the horror of pollution. Seneca also makes the tearing out of the eyes particularly gruesome (Oedipus, 962–70). Jocasta's recognition follows Oedipus's (rather than preceding it, as in Sophocles), and she kills herself onstage, plunging a sword into her body with the cry, "Seek this womb here, O my right hand, the spacious womb that bore both husband and children" (Oedipus, 1038–39).

As Oedipus leaves Thebes for exile, the brighter sky promises an end to the plague (*Oedipus*, 1052–61). Here Seneca, like Sophocles, draws on ancient rituals of the expulsion of the scapegoat (see Chapter 5) and the role of the king as the sacred mediator between the human and supernatural worlds. But his combination of psychology, horror, and the subterranean world—although effective in its own terms—dissolves the subtle Sophoclean relations between character, chance, and destiny. Instead he makes Oedipus an innocent victim of a remote, incomprehensible, and malevolent fate on the one hand and a Stoic hero-king who endures his suffering to save his city on the other.

Seneca's *Phoenician Women* (*Phoenissae*) is a fragmentary work of some 650 lines, the first half of which shows Oedipus in exile, accompanied by his daughter, Antigone, as in *Oedipus at Colonus*. Unlike Sophocles' hero, however, this Oedipus is still tormented by guilt and troubled by visions of Laius's ghost. He feels that he did too little in tearing out his eyes, and he expresses this sentiment in typical Senecan hyperbole: "Now dip your hand into your brain and there complete the death that I began to die" (*Phoenician Women*, 180–81).

Although the oldest surviving manuscript of Seneca's tragedies dates from around 1100, these plays did not become popular until the Renaissance. Then they served as a model for how to adapt the political, intellectual, and ritual elements of an ancient Greek play to modern situations. Seneca's psychological direction remained influential, and he appealed to tastes of the sixteenth and seventeenth centuries for long rhetorical descriptions, hyperbole, melodrama, violence, and supernatural effects. Laius's ghost, possibly Seneca's invention (though with ample precedent, from Aeschylus through Ovid), was to have a long and happy life on the stage.

SEVENTEENTH AND EIGHTEENTH CENTURIES

From the sixteenth century on, as *Oedipus Tyrannus* becomes established as *the* classical tragedy, the number of translations and adaptations increase, and interest in the play is stimulated also by the so-called quarrel between the ancients and the moderns, the ongoing debate about whether the ancient or the contemporary authors are superior. Three plays are particularly important in this period, Corneille's *Oedipe* of 1659, Dryden and Lee's *Oedipus* of 1678, and Voltaire's *Oedipe* of 1718.

All three basically follow Sophocles' plot but add touches from Seneca (e.g. the ghost of Laius appears in both Corneille and Dryden). Theater and theatergoing in seventeenth-century London or Paris was, of course, radically different from what it was in ancient Greece. In his preface Corneille observes that "what had passed for marvelous in their centuries [that is, in Sophocles' and Seneca's time] could seem horrible to ours," and that the long description of Oedipus's blinding in the ancient versions would disturb "the delicacy of our ladies, and their disgust easily brings with it that of the rest of the audience," and so he decided to conceal "such a dangerous spectacle and introduce the happy episode of Theseus and Dirce"—that is, a love story as subplot. Dryden and Voltaire adopted this addition, on the assumption that the Sophoclean recognition plot alone would not interest their audiences.

All three writers transform Sophocles' civic setting into a royal court of their own times, eliminate the chorus, and greatly reduce the role of supernatural and ritual elements, like Delphi, the oracles, Teiresias, and the gods. The action becomes more naturalistic (though still rather stiff by modern standards), and there is more emphasis on the dignity of kingship, on the endurance of fate, and on duty. Although some sense of the sacred power of kingship and the sacred body of the king remains, especially in Corneille and Voltaire, these works have little of Sophocles' idea of an invisible and mysterious mythic order, expressed through the choruses.

Dryden and Lee's complicated play is the most Senecan of the three, with dire omens, Laius's ghost, and many dead bodies onstage at the end. In addition to the erotic subplot, there is also an evil villain, the misshapen Creon, borrowed from Shakespeare's *Richard III*, and Oedipus's disturbed sleepwalking in act 2 borrowed from *Macbeth*. Dryden and Lee's greatest innovation is the insistence on the attraction of the mother and son for one another. Act 1, for example, ends with the couple's profession of their deep love. When Jocasta remarks on the resemblance between Laius and Oedipus, Oedipus says, "No pious son e're loved his Mother more / Than I my dear Jocasta." She replies,

I love you too
The self same way. . . .
For I love Laius still as wives should love:
But you more tenderly; as part of me:
And when I have you in my arms, methinks
I lull my child asleep.

Dryden and Lee also rival Seneca in the goriness of the self-blinding
(act 5, scene 1) but outdo him in the horror of the ending. Jocasta
murders her four children before killing herself, and Oedipus hurls
himself to his death from the tower where he was imprisoned.

Voltaire, whose *Letters on Oedipus* criticized Sophocles' play for
its improbabilities, tries to improve on Corneille by limiting the
subplot, by placing Laius's death just four years in the past, and by
having Oedipus and Jocasta married for only two years. This last
device makes the failure to investigate Laius's death less problematic, reduces the age difference between the royal couple, and
eliminates the horror of the incestuously born children—a particularly troubling aspect of the myth that can be traced back to the
sixth or seventh century B.C. Voltaire's ending combines Seneca
and Corneille: Oedipus remains a good, dutiful king in control of
his emotions and concerned with his people, whom he saves from
the plague with the blood of his mutilated eyes. Jocasta closes the
play with her suicide, complaining against the cruelty of fate.

Voltaire's *Oedipe* remained highly popular on the Parisian
stage, a testimony to the power of the myth but also to the decorum
and rationality of Voltaire's treatment. It led to a spate of further
imitations. One version, that of Antoine Houdar de la Motte (1754),
has Laius's servant, out of cowardice, tell the lie that the old king is
killed by a lion, so that Oedipus is completely thrown off the track
and has no reason to suspect that he might be the killer.

NINETEENTH AND TWENTIETH CENTURIES

From the sixteenth to the eighteenth century imitators of *Oedipus
Tyrannus* emphasize the Senecan motif of fate rather than the
Sophoclean concern with knowledge and self-discovery. Thus they
placed more emphasis on Oedipus's ability to accept his suffering

with nobility and strength than on his determination to search out
truth in a world of illusion. On the other hand, the continuing concern with kingship enabled Corneille, Dryden, and Voltaire to
develop the more public aspect of Sophocles' play. They introduced
a mob made restless and hostile by the plague, dynastic conflicts
and palace intrigue, the themes of authority, lineage, succession,
and the sacrificial act that brings salvation at the end.

The numerous nineteenth- and twentieth-century versions are
more concerned with personal and philosophical themes: the
meaning of existence, the individual's alienation from the world and
himself, the mystery of individual destiny, the incestuous attraction. Freud, whose reading is discussed in Chapter 5, dominates
every view of the myth after him, although there are foreshadowings
of his interpretation in the combination of incest, madness, and
heredity in the Oedipal elements of Ibsen's *Ghosts* (1882) and, as
we have noted, even in Dryden and Lee. *Oedipus Tyrannus* is by
now famous enough to invite parody, as in Percy Bysshe Shelley's
satirical beast-parable, *Oedipus Tyrannus; or, Swellfoot the Tyrant*,
and August von Platen's *Der romantische Oedipus* (1828). A freer
adaptation is Heinrich von Kleist's comedy *The Broken Jar* (*Der
zerbrochene Krug*, performed in 1808), which combines the Oedipal
rivalry between an older and younger lover of the same woman with
the motifs of judicial investigation, disguise, and reversal from
magistrate to criminal. In a darker mood, Friedrich von Schiller's
Bride of Messina (1803) fuses the deadly rivalry of the two brothers
in *Oedipus at Colonus* with a version of *Oedipus Tyrannus* in which
the dread oracle about the birth of the king's child concerns a
daughter rather than a son. Each of the two brothers, ignorant of
their sister's identity, falls in love with her, with disastrous results
for the royal house. *Oedipus Tyrannus's* family violence is thus
made to take place a generation later and is transformed to
brother-sister incest.

The German Romantic poet Friedrich Hölderlin produced a
powerful though stilted verse translation of *Oedipus Tyrannus*,
Oedipus der Tyrann, along with an *Antigone* (both in 1804). His
translation boldly catches much of the Sophoclean grandeur, state-
liness, and poetic imagery. More controversial are his "Notes on the
Oedipus" ("Anmerkungen zum Oedipus") appended to the translation, which, along with the similar "Notes on the *Antigone*," attempt

to develop a theory of tragedy. Here *Oedipus* is the model for the tragic individual's confrontation with ultimate reality. He is torn from his normal sphere of life, pulled between the extremes of the human and the divine, and led destructively into the merciless light of the absolute. Hölderlin is elliptical and cryptic, and despite the enthusiasm of Heidegger, critics have been divided about whether the "Notes" were the product of the poet's genius or the signs of the insanity that ended his creative life in 1804. Genius has been the dominant view recently. In any case, Hölderlin helped to establish the Romantic view of *Oedipus Tyrannus* that has strongly influenced recent interpretation—namely approaching the play in terms of the metaphysical questions of ultimate reality, the paradoxes of identity, the intersection of human and divine, and the hero's total isolation in a world of mysterious and remote powers.

The Romantic interpretation is expressed rather more clearly in an 11 November 1815 letter from the philosopher Schopenhauer to the poet Goethe:

> It is the courage to search problems through to the end that makes the philosopher. He must be like Sophocles' Oedipus, who, in seeking to illuminate his terrible destiny, pursues his quest untiringly, even when he realizes that the answer holds only horror and terror for him. But most of us carry in their hearts a Jocasta who begs Oedipus for the love of the gods not to investigate further.

Here the emphasis falls not only on Oedipus's search for the truth but also on the special destiny of this search that sets him apart from ordinary, more complacent people (Jocasta).

At the end of the Romantic tradition stands Hugo von Hofmannsthal's *Oedipus and the Sphinx* (1905), planned as part of a trilogy that was never completed. Hofmannsthal's is a very metaphysical Oedipus who swings between nothingness and godhead, despair and exaltation. At the opening he is in suicidal desperation, having abandoned his entire past life when he heard Apollo's terrible oracle at Delphi. Hofmannsthal's post-Romantic lyricism combines a mystical with a psychological tone. The god's oracle is delivered through the intermediary of an alluring female figure, a mother/lover, who will awaken Oedipus to his true identity. The voice of the god, or fate, is thus interpreted in highly personal and inward terms: it holds the secret of the alienated hero's still-invisible strength and his ultimate purpose in the world. Oedipus defeats the Sphinx in an eerie setting, where the struggle is with his own self-doubt and despair rather than with knowledge or monstrosity. The play ends in an ecstatic union between the victorious hero, who seems reborn virtually as a god, and the queen, who is fascinated by his godlike power and beauty. The atmosphere is one of foreboding, mystical visions, and confused desires; self-destructive violence alternates with feelings of limitless power and godlike bliss. We are closer here to Freud than to Sophocles.

The *Oedipe* of André Gide (1930) and *The Infernal Machine* of Jean Cocteau (1934) are perhaps the best known adaptations of *Oedipus Tyrannus* in this century. In contrast to the high lyrical and mystical tone of Hofmannsthal, Gide and Cocteau bring the myth down to earth with an irreverent, tragicomic mixture of the mythical and the everyday and with a lot of talk, spiced with Gallic wit. They also take the opposite tack from Corneille and Voltaire: rather than gloss over the horrors (or giving them symbolic and mystical meaning, as did Hofmannsthal) they set them out fully into a harsh, ironic light. Gide's Jocasta knows the truth all along and tries to persuade Oedipus to keep it as a secret between them when he learns it.[5] Gide also adds an incestuous attraction between Oedipus's sons and their sister, Ismene, to parallel the father's incestuous marriage. Cocteau's entire third act takes place on Oedipus and Jocasta's wedding night in the queen's bedroom, where she keeps a cradle at the foot of the bed to remind her of her lost child, and there are many references to the mother-son relation that mysteriously draws the two together in their love.

Gide's Oedipus is a kind of existentialist hero. He exults in being a bastard, since that leaves him free to form his own identity. Gide reinterprets the myth, and especially the incest motif, in terms of a debate between absolute freedom and the restraints of law, society, and religion. Oedipus is a seeker after truth and an independent, freethinking spirit. His authenticity contrasts with Teiresias's self-righteous piety, Creon's self-serving greed, and Jocasta's willingness to compromise for the sake of a comfortable bourgeois happiness.

Gide's play is more black comedy than tragedy, and it often calls attention to its outrageousness in compressing or parodying the original. In the debate between Oedipus and Teiresias in act 1, for example, the chorus intervenes colloquially, "It's no good, Oedipus, it's no good. You know very well that with Teiresias even a King can't have the last word."6 Gide's Ismene is a precocious teenager, and Antigone wants to be a nun. The self-blinding at the end is not so much an act of horror and remorse as one of desperate courage in refusing the veil of ignorant happiness that Jocasta would live with.

In *The Infernal Machine* Cocteau creates a counterpoint between his light, contemporary mood and the mythic seriousness of the original with the device of "the Voice" that introduces each act and replaces the Sophoclean gods. This Voice opens the play with a synopsis of the story and, directly addressing the spectator, describes the plot as a diabolical construction "by the infernal gods for the mathematical destruction of a mortal."7

Taking a hint from Dryden (and indirectly from Seneca), Cocteau begins the action with a *Hamlet*-like scene of Laius's ghost on the castle walls trying to warn Jocasta of the impending danger. Jocasta, a spoiled and fun-loving socialite, visits the battlements, accompanied by her well-meaning, devoted, but somewhat bumbling priest, Teiresias, whom she affectionately calls Zizi. Cocteau draws on both Freud and the Surrealists for his third act, which takes place on the wedding night. Oedipus and Jocasta each dreams some aspect of the truth but cannot quite grasp it consciously. Indeed, they have just the conversation that readers of *Oedipus* often wonder about: Jocasta talks of her lost child, and Oedipus gives an account of the scars on his feet.

Cocteau's ending draws on the mood of *Oedipus at Colonus.* Jocasta's ghost, invisible to everyone except Oedipus, reclaims him as her lost child and joins with Antigone to lead him on his journey to truth. Teiresias returns at the end, speaking the voice of posterity, to free Oedipus from Creon's authority. He declares that he belongs to "the people, to the poets, to the pure in heart." The line is perhaps Cocteau's antidote to his irreverent treatment, suggesting that the great ancient myths have a universal power and, through the modernized form that Cocteau adopts, still have something important to tell us, but they can speak only in a kind of cool, self-deprecating irony, or, as one critic says, "as though through the din of a cocktail party, he were endeavoring in secret asides to tell a fairy story to a child."[8]

VISUAL AND MUSICAL ARTS: RECENT ADAPTATIONS

In addition to its various literary adaptations, *Oedipus Tyrannus* has had a long life in painting and music. The best known paintings are probably the monumental canvasses depicting Oedipus and the Sphinx by Jean-Auguste-Dominique Ingres (1808) and Gustave Moreau (1864), now in the Louvre and the Metropolitan Museum in New York, respectively. Ingres's Sphinx stands on a rock above Oedipus, surrounded by the limbs and skeletons of her victims. The narrow defile suggests the hero's passage through a dangerous trial, between death or rebirth. A man in the background looks on with a gesture of amazement or fear. Moreau retains Ingres's ghastly landscape but transforms the meeting into a deadly, quasi-erotic embrace in which the outcome looks dubious for the hero. The play has inspired many lesser works, of which the most curious is perhaps Max Ernst's surrealist *Oedipus Rex* (1922), now in a private collection in Paris, in which the piercing of Oedipus's ankles in infancy may be suggested by two gigantic fingers that project from a darkened window and are transfixed by a large and shiny metal pin.

There have been musical settings or accompaniments of the myth ever since Gabrieli's choruses for the 1585 premier of *Oedipus Tyrannus* in Vicenza. Jean-Baptiste Lully wrote a ballet for Corneille's *Oedipe* in 1664, and Henry Purcell wrote the music to the Dryden and Lee *Oedipus* in 1678. Rossini, Schubert, Mendelssohn, and Mussorgsky have all written music on the Oedipus theme. The Italian composer Ruggiero Leoncavallo wrote an opera, *Edipo Re*, which was first performed in 1920, the year after his death; and in 1928 Igor Stravinsky produced a rather static oratorio version, *Oedipus Rex*, with a Latin text written (originally in French) by Cocteau. For the 1984 musical *Gospel at Colonus*, Bob Telson and Lee Breuer adapted *Oedipus at Colonus* to a Christian framework in an African-American setting.

29

Oedipus and the Sphinx, 1808. Jean-Auguste-Dominique Ingres. Louvre, Paris. *Photograph courtesy of Giraudon/Art Resource, New York City.*

Oedipus and the Sphinx, 1864. Gustave Moreau. Bequest of William H. Herriman, 1921 (21.134.1). Metropolitan Museum of Art, New York City.

The Italian director Pier Paolo Pasolini produced a film version, *Edipo Re*, in 1967. Like Cocteau's *Infernal Machine*, it is highly psychological, with a heavy Freudian emphasis on the mother-son incest. Pasolini tries to suggest the universality of the Oedipus complex by telling the story in three different settings: ancient Thebes (for the dominant part of the film), a vaguely nineteenth-century village in southern Italy and a contemporary industrial city. He tells the story biographically, from Oedipus's birth to his blinding and its aftermath, but makes heavy use of the Sophoclean text when he comes to the plague at Thebes. His Oedipus is an impulsive, passionate, sensual man, with little of the searcher-after-truth about him. Instead, the film lingers on the sexual attraction between Oedipus and the queen. It links the crime and the punishment not only by using Jocasta's huge brooch as the instrument of Oedipus's self-blinding, but also by focusing on the brooch in the several earlier scenes of lovemaking in the marital bed.

The film tries to make up for its lack of philosophical depth by exploiting an anthropological fascination with the primitive, and Pasolini shows in graphic detail the horrors that Sophocles removes to narration only. There are imaginative and powerful visual realizations of the Sophoclean material, however, in the exposure of the infant, in Oedipus's consultation of the Delphic oracle, in the questioning of Teiresias, and especially in the sequence in which the young, exhausted, confused Oedipus tries to run away from the encounter with Laius and then, with an infusion of some demonic energy from a hidden source, turns back to kill the servants and the old king.

The film has a certain raw, bitter power as a depiction of an unaccountable disaster that overwhelms innocent, puzzled, and helpless people. It reinterprets Sophocles in terms of the meaninglessness and alienation of modern life. This Oedipus at the end is not taught by suffering or heroized by his passage through the limits of human endurance, as is the Oedipus of *Oedipus at Colonus*, but is simply a blind young man lost and adrift in an impersonal modern metropolis.

In modern literature nearly every major poet has, at some time or another, drawn on an aspect of the Oedipus legend as a meditation on the human condition. Among them are Jorge Luis Borges, Richard Eberhart, William Empson, Randall Jarrell, Stanley Kunitz,

Archibald MacLeish, James Merrill, Edwin Muir, Edith Sitwell, Stephen Spender, Alan Tate, and William Butler Yeats. Among novelists, Alain Robbe-Grillet in *The Erasers* (1953) and Thomas Pynchon in *The Crying of Lot 49* (1967)—with its character Mrs. Oedipa Maas—draw more or less explicitly on the plot structure of *Oedipus Tyrannus*.[9] Edward Bond's *Saved* (1985) recasts the story into a version that prevents the parricide. The French writer Hélène Cixous produced an operatic version in 1978, *Le nom d'Oedipe: chant du corps interdit (The Name of Oedipus: Song of the Forbidden Body)*, focusing on the incestuous relation between Oedipus and Jocasta.

Teiresias has taken on a literary life of his own, from Ovid's account of his transformation into a woman and back again (*Metamorphoses* [ca. A.D. 8], book 3), to T. S. Eliot's *The Waste Land* (1922), in which he is the prophet of a truth more prosaic than that of *Oedipus Tyrannus*: "I, Teiresias, though blind, throbbing between two lives, / Old man with wrinkled female breasts, can see."[10] Eliot also adapted *Oedipus at Colonus* in his late play *The Elder Statesman* (1958), in which the Furies are the old man's guilty memories of unsavory acts in his past, exorcized by confession and love.

Contemporary writers continue to find in the myth symbols and images that speak to a wide range of modern issues. In Alberto Moravia's play *Il Dio Kurt (The God Kurt,* ca. 1948), a German commander artificially creates an Oedipus drama as part of the barbarity of his concentration camp. Writers in the Muslim world, in Africa, and in Bali have adapted the play to their local settings.[11] Muriel Rukeyser, in her poem "Myth," finally has the Sphinx turn the tables on Oedipus. Her Sphinx is a female voice demanding to be heard in its own right, after centuries of enduring "Man" as the only answer to the riddle.

LITERARY CRITICISM TODAY

As the reception of *Oedipus Tyrannus* over some 25 centuries shows, every age reads its legacy from the past in terms of its own needs, concerns, and experiences. As one would expect, the cataclysms and nuclear and environmental threats of the past 50 years and the consequent weakening of traditional religious and philosophical belief in a beneficent universe have affected the way today's critics view Greek tragedy. Contemporary interpreters see *Oedipus Tyrannus*, and Greek tragedy in general, as an expression of doubt and anguish rather than of piety, a questioning of meaning rather than an assertion of meaning. Post–World War II critics are thus less inclined to explain Oedipus's suffering by a "tragic flaw" of anger or pride, and relatively few regard the play as the triumph of an equitable divine order.

Interpreters of *Oedipus Tyrannus* and of Sophocles generally over the past four or five decades can be divided into those who emphasize the hero and those who emphasize the gods. We may label these the *humanists* and the *theologizers*, respectively, or, as some have suggested, the hero-worshipers and the pietists. The humanistic view, eloquently represented by Cedric Whitman in *Sophocles: A Study of Heroic Humanism* (1951), has Oedipus as an individual of heroic grandeur and remarkable energy and courage. Despite the cruel trick that life and the gods play on him, he has an unflinching determination to learn the truth about himself and the strength to live with that terrible truth when its horror is revealed.

Bernard Knox, in *The Heroic Temper* (1964) and, to a lesser extent, in his *Oedipus at Thebes* (1957), develops a darker version of the humanistic view. The focus is still on the hero, but his integrity and unyielding devotion to ideals of honor and dignity have another side in stubborn self-centeredness, transgressive overreaching, dangerous overconfidence, and vengefulness. Powerful loyalty and commitment can engender strong hatred and fierce bitterness. Rather than serving as a model of excellence or virtue (*aretè*), the hero is a puzzle and a problem. His independence and greatness of spirit are of the same fabric as his egotism, narrow intransigence, and tendency to excess and violence. The Greek heroes Ajax, Electra, and Philoctetes are perhaps the clearest examples, but we can see some of these traits in Oedipus too.

According to the theological view, the heart of *Oedipus Tyrannus* is not the hero as much as the vision of the gods and the world order that emerges from the play's action. For moralistic interpreters, of whom the best known is perhaps C. M. Bowra in his *Sophoclean Tragedy* (1944), Oedipus is guilty of terrible crimes, and the gods cause his downfall to illustrate their enforcement of moral laws. Oedipus himself is a model of the fragility of human happiness and the precariousness of human life in general.

A very different theological orientation appears in E. R. Dodds's celebrated article, "On Misunderstanding the *Oedipus Rex*" (1966), and in R. P. Winnington-Ingram's book, *Sophocles: An Interpretation* (1980). Dodds and Winnington-Ingram agree that Oedipus's acts violate the laws of gods and men but stress that he is morally and legally innocent. His downfall illustrates a world order whose workings do not square with human conceptions of justice. The tragic dimension of the play lies precisely in the gap between the remote, incomprehensible gods and any sense of humanly meaningful suffering. Sophocles' traditional piety is not to be understood as a complacent acceptance of beneficent gods but rather as a recognition of the inscrutable and mysterious "other" in divinities who exist in a far-off realm untouched by age, change, or time.

Not all of these positions are mutually incompatible. Winnington-Ingram, for instance, provides an interesting synthesis of Knox's darker heroism and a theological interpretation of Sophocles. What makes life tragic in Sophocles' view, he suggests (to simplify a little), is the way human nature and the gods interact to produce suffering for mankind. Tragedy occurs when character and events converge so that men destroy themselves and those closest to them, despite and sometimes because of their best qualities.

The richness of *Oedipus Tyrannus* is such that all of the interpretations described, and many other permutations and combinations, are defensible. This is not because Sophocles could not tell us clearly and precisely what he wanted to say. Rather, he condensed into a single work the problem of the meaning of existence, focused on one strong, vivid personality, and he presented this with the balance and complexity the task required. If scholars continue to differ over the meaning of the play, it is also because intelligent and sensitive men and women continue to differ over the meaning of life.

4

Performance, Theater, and Social Context

DRAMA AT THE FESTIVALS OF DIONYSUS

In ancient Greece dramas were performed each year in Athens as part of the festival of Dionysus, the god of wine, vegetation, religious ecstasy, the mask, and the theater. Actually, two festivals included dramatic performances: the Lenaea, which took place at the end of January, and the Great or City Dionysia, which took place at the end of March and lasted for five or six days. The Great Dionysia was by far the more important. Tragedies were introduced at the Lenaea relatively late in the history of Athenian theater, probably in the 430s.

During the festival of the Dionysia, all male citizens and possibly (but not certainly) their wives would gather to watch 12 plays by three tragedians; each dramatist presented three tragedies and a satyr play. There were also five (later three) comedies, and choral performances of dithyrambs (hymns in honor of Dionysus) sung and danced by men and boys. The plays to be performed were selected by a magistrate in a preliminary competition held some months before the festival. At the festival itself five judges were selected by lot to award first, second, and third prizes.

The performances took place in the great open-air theater of Dionysus, which was built into the hillside in the precinct of the god, on the southern slope of the Acropolis, where it can be visited today. The plays began at dawn and continued throughout the day.

36

The crowd sat on wooden benches like bleachers. Not until the fourth century B.C. were the stone benches built that survive today in the remains of the theaters at Athens, Epidaurus, Delphi, and elsewhere in Greece, Asia Minor, and Sicily. By the time of *Oedipus Tyrannus* the festivals of Dionysus were famous, and many foreigners, especially from Athens's subject allies, would attend. Plays were performed only once, at the Dionysiac festivals, although in some cases there would be repeat performances at lesser Dionysiac festivals in the smaller towns outside of Athens. There were no private theaters or private companies. The performances were financed by the state, with the help of wealthy citizens' contributions for the cost of outfitting and training the chorus.

The festival was simultaneously a religious and a civic occasion. It began with a procession in honor of Dionysus, and various state functions also took place in the theater: the pouring of libations to the gods by the 10 elected generals; the display of the tribute from Athens's subjects; the uniformed parade of young soldiers who had been brought up at public expense because their fathers had been killed in war; and the reading of the names and honors of those who had benefited the city.[1] The audience, therefore, was prepared to see a representation of events that had significance for the life of the community, especially in its relation to the gods, to public as well as private morality, and to the world order in general.

Staging the plays was simple. The circular performance area, into which the audience looked from above, was backed by a long, low building (the scene building or *skene*) with a slightly raised platform in front of it. Characters entered and exited through the front door of the scene building, which in *Oedipus Tyrannus* represents Oedipus's palace. The building's roof could also serve as the place where a divinity could appear as the deus ex machina—a device rare in Sophocles and not used in any of the Theban plays—to end the play.

The chorus danced in the circular performance area in front of the scene building, called the orchestra or "dancing place." There was easy communication between the orchestra and the low platform behind it on which the actors stood. There was probably an altar of Dionysus in the center of the orchestra. In the opening scene of *Oedipus Tyrannus* this altar was probably the gathering place for the procession of suppliants. It should be noted that there are no stage directions in our texts; we have to infer all stage action from the play itself, and many details of Sophocles' staging remain uncertain.

By modern standards, the stage was bare. There were few props. All the roles were played by male actors, who wore stylized masks and elaborate costumes. Only three actors per play were allowed, and they took different roles. Thus the actor who plays Creon in the first half of *Oedipus Tyrannus* returns later in the role of the Corinthian Messenger, and the actor who plays Jocasta returns as the Herdsman after Jocasta exits for her suicide. There were also supernumeraries for nonspeaking roles, like the suppliants in the opening scene of *Oedipus* or the guard whom Oedipus tells to bind the Herdsman. The 15-member chorus remained onstage during the entire performance and could interact with the actors like a regular character; at these times the chorus leader, or *koryphaios*, spoke for the whole chorus. The odes, sung by the chorus as a whole, were accompanied by the *aulos*, a reed instrument more like our oboe than a flute, and the chorus also danced in accompaniment to these songs.

With the exception of a small bit of music for a chorus of Euripides' *Orestes*, all the music and choreography of Greek drama are lost. Every tragedy is composed in verse, and the language is lofty and poetic. The lyrics of the choral odes tend to be even more elaborate than the dialogue, and they often pose serious problems of interpretation because of their figurative language, abrupt leaps of thought, metaphors, and highly allusive style. The dialogue is written in a meter known as iambic trimeter, which consists of six iambic feet. It is a supple meter, and it allowed the tragedian both to approximate the rhythms of ordinary speech and to attain a dignity above the everyday. The effect is analogous to the blank verse in Elizabethan drama or the Alexandrines in the classic French drama of Corneille and Racine.

Each play was performed from beginning to end without intermission. There was no curtain and no formal division into acts or scenes. The choral odes, at more or less regular intervals, mark pauses in the action; they often follow a crisis or climax, and thus they allow us to absorb what has happened and to reflect on the meaning of the events. Sophocles generally began his plays by showing his main characters in action in the prologue, the section before the entrance of the chorus. The chorus members then entered from the wings at either side of the scene building to sing their first ode, known as the parode or *parodos*. Subsequent odes are called *stasima* (singular, *stasimon*). As noted, these were danced as well as sung and so had a solemn, ritualized effect. Indeed, the choruses themselves often consisted in ritual actions like prayers to the gods, as is the case in the first ode of *Oedipus Tyrannus*.

The chorus is perhaps the hardest feature of Greek drama for modern readers to appreciate, just as it is the most perplexing for modern stage directors. It is a mistake to assume that the chorus is the mouthpiece of the playwright. Its statements are not to be taken at face value as an independent view of reality. The chorus, as Aristotle explained long ago, is a dramatic element, an actor among other actors. It shows us the communal background of the action, which is essential to *Oedipus Tyrannus* and to every other Greek play. Greek tragedy assumes that no life is entirely private—that the city's fortunes are inextricable from the individual's, and vice versa.

The chorus is so important to the play because Greek tragedy, unlike its modern counterpart, is a public art form. It is not just about individual lives; it reflects on such issues as the nature of authority, justice, the worship of the gods. And it does so in a wide framework of symbolic discourse made possible by myth, which connects matters of ethical and political life with questions about the world order on the one hand and more personal matters—relations between the sexes, tensions within the family, generational conflicts, the pull between public and private or between civic responsibility and individual desires or between family life and politics—on the other. The tragedy combines a public language of moral generalization and ritualized expressions of communal sentiment (generally by the chorus) within unusual (though not necessarily atypical) situations of personal emotion and intimate private life.

The chorus's collective response complements the individual responses of the main characters, but its response is not privileged just because it is collective. The chorus can be indecisive, as in Aeschylus's *Agamemnon*, or cowardly, as in Sophocles' *Electra*; it can turn murderous, as in Euripides' *Bacchae*; and it can even lie and enter into deception, as in Sophocles' *Philoctetes*. In *Oedipus Tyrannus* it shows us, first of all, the terrible sufferings that result from the hidden pollution, in the effects of the plague. Then, as the play goes on, the chorus is a vehicle for various hypotheses about what the events might mean and a sounding board for the emotions that they arouse.

Aristotle praises Sophocles for making his chorus participate directly in the action, in contrast to the more detached chorus of Euripides (*Poetics*, 18.1456a). In *Oedipus Tyrannus* Sophocles certainly uses the chorus to show the city's reactions to the events of the play, for example in its response to Oedipus's curse on the murderer of Laius (276–95) and later in its reaction to Oedipus's suffering after he blinds himself (1296–1368).

The odes are always in character and so contain sentiments appropriate to the elderly citizens of Thebes. On the other hand, their intricate poetry and imagery often suggest more than the chorus itself knows and introduce a perspective that reaches beyond the human limitations of any single character. The odes of *Oedipus Tyrannus* contain no myths and almost no narrative (the only exception is the brief allusion to Oedipus's defeat of the Sphinx [507–10]). But they remind us constantly of the forces of nature outside the city, of the gods and their cults and oracles, and of the need to understand the suffering of Thebes and of Oedipus in a wider philosophical and religious context.

THE MYTHICAL MATERIAL OF GREEK TRAGEDY

With a few exceptions, the classical Greek tragedians drew their plots from a body of inherited, traditional tales about gods and heroes that had taken shape gradually over many centuries. Most of these stories are about figures of the remote Mycenaean culture, the great Bronze Age civilization that flourished in Greece from about 1600 to about 1200 B.C. Agamemnon, Achilles, Ajax, Oedipus, Theseus, to take the most prominent, are legendary kings of great Mycenaean cities. The exact date when the stories about them took shape cannot be determined with certainty, but it is probable that they were handed down from generation to generation in an oral tradition—modified, embellished, and endlessly varied—from the time of the disintegration of Mycenaean civilization in the twelfth century B.C. to the beginnings of the Greek city-state in the middle of the eighth century B.C. These tales then continued to form the material of the epic and lyric poetry of the early Greek city-state, as we see in Homer's *Iliad* and *Odyssey*, Hesiod's *Theogony* and *Works and Days*, and Pindar's *Victory Odes*.

This is a culture of song, performance, and oral recitation rather than of the written word. Indeed, books are relatively rare before the end of the fifth century B.C. Because an oral culture has little concern for a fixed text, it also has no notion that a given myth must have one and only one definitive form. The bards would sing their mythic tales with many possible variants from performance to performance; different versions coexisted from city to city and even within the same city. Hence, as we shall see, there are numerous variants in the myth of Oedipus.

In addition to the considerable body of epic and choral poetry that recounted the myths, sculptors and painters illustrated these stories, though to what extent they added their own interpretations and modifications is controversial. The pediments and metopes of the temples, terra-cotta tablets, sarcophagi, bronzes, and particularly the innumerable vases show how pervasive myths were in this culture. As literary sources are often lost or fragmentary, these visual representations offer important evidence for early versions of the myths.

The myths had many functions in the cultural life of archaic and classical Greece (the period from approximately 750 to 350 B.C.). At a time when there was no other form of historical record, they were the repository of the past and retained the memory of great events and noteworthy deeds. These tales also embodied the values and concerns central to the society. The Homeric epics in particular provided models for heroic behavior and the ideal warrior and ruler, especially in an aristocratic society. Analogously, the tragedies, presented to the entire citizen body at the great civic festivals, were not just a major event in Athenian cultural life but were also a kind of mirror in which the city could view itself from the perspective of the whole heroic tradition and the values, ideals, and modes of behavior crystallized in the myths.

41

The tragedians were mythmakers and storytellers as well as playwrights. They continued the work of Homer and Hesiod, speculating on the questions of the world order, divine justice, and human nature through their own versions of the ancient tales. They are thus part of the venerable tradition that runs from the *Iliad* through the *Argonautica* of Apollonius of Rhodes in the third century B.C. and on to Virgil's *Aeneid* and Ovid's *Metamorphoses* in the early Roman Empire. Neither they nor the poets who preceded them were interested in creating fictions; they preferred the traditional tales, with their centuries of encrusted meaning and authority.[2] The tragedies' mythical material gave them a perspective, seriousness, and universality comparable, say, to the historical themes of the Elizabethan theater. The grandeur and heroic elevation of the material were sustained by the lofty poetry, the elaborate costumes, and the intricate performance in dance and song by the chorus.

The convention of using mythical plots may seem constraining to us, but it probably did not feel so to a poet working in a highly traditional society whose members were accustomed to think in terms of the images and symbols of mythical narration. The tragedian could count on an informed and trained audience, and this fact doubtless contributed to the extraordinarily high quality of the works we have. During the great flowering of drama in fifth-century Athens, nearly 1,000 tragedies were performed at the Great Dionysia, but of these only 33 survive complete. The audiences at the plays would know at least the outline of the plot, and they would both understand and delight in the special twists that each playwright gave his version. Many spectators, for example, knowing Aeschylus's plays, would appreciate Sophocles' innovations and understand why he told his Oedipus story in the way that he did.

TRAGEDY AND DEMOCRACY IN ATHENS

Drama was invented when the mythical tales were not just recited (as was the case with epic) but were acted out by living figures on the stage. This innovation is attributed to an obscure Athenian named Thespis and seems to have occurred in Athens at the very end of the sixth century B.C. It meant a quantum leap in the immediacy and power with which the myths were felt by an audience. The new form was particularly well suited to the Athenian democracy, which began in the 490s, since the theater can publicly explore ethical and political controversies and reflect on the most urgent issues of the times. In adapting to a democratic audience the ancient tales about kings and proud aristocratic warriors obsessed with power, honor, and vengeance, the tragic poets transformed them radically. This recasting of myth into dramatic form was unique to Athens, and it is surely not a coincidence that the democracy and the drama begin at about the same time.

By utilizing a structure of opposing characters, protagonist and antagonist, tragedy focuses the myths more sharply on conflict, on opposing principles and definitions, on questions of individual choice and responsibility, on the clash between public and private good and between competitive and cooperative virtues, and on the problem of the man of exceptional greatness in an egalitarian ideology. Both Aeschylus's *Seven against Thebes* and Sophocles' *Oedipus Tyrannus*, for example, open with a crisis for the city in which a leader standing before his citizens bears the responsibility for taking decisive action. Such situations would naturally appeal to an audience accustomed to seeing every major decision, whether political, legal, or financial, hammered out in debates and adversarial speeches in the assembly and the law courts.

The political context of Athenian drama (as indeed of all of Greek literature) is important for understanding the form, and we shall see its implications for *Oedipus Tyrannus*. When we go to the theater today we expect an evening of private entertainment at a place and time of our choosing; in ancient Athens to go to the theater was to participate in a civic festival and to join with all of one's fellow citizens in probing the big questions of justice and injustice, evil and its punishment, social responsibility, the nature of the gods, the meaning of suffering. These are the issues that become the material of philosophy in the next century, but before the age of prose they still belonged to the poets. Plato, who writes his dialogues in dramatic form, is in a sense the successor to the tragedians in a postmythical age.

5

The Oedipus Myth and
Its Interpretation

THE MYTH BEFORE SOPHOCLES

The myth of Oedipus is very old and formed part of a series (or cycle) of epics about Thebes. In *Works and Days* (composed between 740 and 700 B.C.) Hesiod refers in passing to the heroes of old who fought "at seven-gated Thebes over the flocks of Oedipus" (ll. 162–63), a possible reference to the struggle between Oedipus's two sons for the throne of Thebes. In the *Iliad* Homer mentions "the grave of Oedipus who had fallen in battle" (23.679–80), a version of the story that suggests that Oedipus continued to rule in Thebes and was honored at his death. Presumably, too, he was not blind.

Our fullest early account of the myth occurs in the *Odyssey*. Odysseus, recounting his adventures in the palace of the Phaeacians, tells how he saw the famous heroines in the underworld, among whom is Jocasta, here called Epicaste:

> And I saw the beautiful Epicaste, Oedipus' mother,
> who in the ignorance of her mind had done a monstrous
> thing and married her own son. He killed his father
> and married her, but the gods soon made it all known to mortals.
> But he, for all his sorrows, in beloved Thebes continued
> to be lord over the Cadmeans, all through the bitter designing
> of the gods; while she went down to Hades of the gates, the strong one,
> knotting a noose and hanging sheer from the high ceiling,

in the constraint of her sorrow, but left to him who survived her
all the sorrows that are brought to pass by a mother's Furies.
(Lattimore's translation, 11.271–80)

This version says nothing about the oracles, the self-blinding, or
the couple's children, but it does give a prominent place to the
gods' intervention, with suggestions of divine malevolence or cruelty. It vividly depicts Jocasta's suffering in the grief that accompa-
nies her suicide, a small anticipation of the tragic form that her
story would find in the hands of the dramatists. The Furies (in
Greek, the *Erinyes*) are dreaded underworld deities who fulfill family curses and are the avengers of murder within the family. Their
presence here does not necessarily mean that Jocasta curses Oedipus at her death, but the family-curse motif is there for Aeschylus
to develop. Homer may have deliberately omitted the incestuously
born children; his epic grandeur tends to shun such ugly details.

The family curse, as we shall see, will be important for
Aeschylus, but it is already prominent in the epics about Thebes,
which were composed between the seventh and fifth centuries B.C.
but perhaps drawn from older material. In these poems Oedipus's
sons, Eteocles and Polyneices, quarrel bitterly over the kingdom of
Thebes when he leaves the throne. Polyneices enlists the help of
Adrastus, king of Argos, and returns to Thebes with six other chiefs
to take the kingdom by force. The expedition fails, and in the attack
the two brothers kill one another at the gates of Thebes. Their fratricidal self-slaughter is the result of a curse from their father.

One of the Theban epics, the *Oedipodeia*, known only from late
summaries and a few fragments, told how Oedipus had his children
by a second wife, Euryganeia; the *Thebais*, also lost, told how
Oedipus cursed his sons in anger because he felt that they dishonored him by giving him a meaner cut of meat at a sacrifice and by
giving him wine in the cup of his murdered father, Laius. A recently
recovered papyrus fragment attributed to the lyric poet Stesichorus
(who flourished in southern Italy around 600 B.C.) contains a
speech in which a mother (presumably Jocasta) tries to dissuade
her sons from civil war by suggesting that one take the kingdom,
the other the movable property.[1] Here too the prophet Teiresias
foretells the sons' doom from oracles of Apollo. This fragment, along

with the passage from the *Odyssey*, again shows the beginnings of the tragic conception of Jocasta that Sophocles will develop.

The most important pre-Sophoclean treatment of the myth is Aeschylus's trilogy of 467 B.C., which comprised *Laius*, *Oedipus*, and *Seven against Thebes*, the last referring to the warriors whom the exiled brother, Polyneices, leads against the city. The accompanying satyr play, *Sphinx*, dramatized Oedipus's victory over that monster. Only *Seven against Thebes* is extant, but references and quotations in later writers provide evidence for the first two plays. In *Laius* Aeschylus probably told the story of Laius's love for Pelops's son, Chrysippus. He carries the boy off, and Chrysippus, in shame, commits suicide, whereupon his father calls down on Laius the curse that eventually destroys his house.[2] Aeschylus traces this curse over the three generations of Laius's family, with one generation per play. His *Oedipus* probably covered much of the same ground as Sophocles' play, and we shall turn to it soon. *Seven* ends with the death of the brothers at each other's hand and the resolve of Antigone to defy Creon's decree forbidding burial of Eteocles (an ending sometimes suspected of having been added to the play much later under the influence of Sophocles' *Antigone* of 442 B.C.).

It is characteristic of the difference between Aeschylus's and Sophocles' Oedipus plays that Aeschylus speaks of the Fury as the "all-true evil prophet" of disaster for the house of Oedipus (*Seven against Thebes*, 720–26), whereas Sophocles has only a passing reference to the Fury, and even here he subordinates supernatural agency to the play of human emotions. The Fury is mentioned at the peak of Teiresias's anger, as he shouts to Oedipus, "The double-smiting, dread-footed curse of your mother and father will drive you from this land" (417–18). The language recalls Aeschylus's *Seven against Thebes* (70, 791), where curse and Fury are closely associated. Sophocles, however, does not mention the Fury by name; he instead emphasizes the oracles and brings their mysterious power onstage in the person of Teiresias, whose mysterious seeing blindness also keeps the problem of knowledge—of how we know—in the foreground.[3]

The only acts common to all the early versions of the myth of Oedipus are the killing of his father and the incestuous marriage. Oedipus's self-blinding appears for the first time in Aeschylus's trilogy and was probably described in his lost *Oedipus*. The chorus in *Seven against Thebes* is probably referring to the preceding play when it tells how Oedipus blinded himself when he became aware of his past:

> But when in misery he knew
> the meaning of his dreadful marriage,
> in pain distraught, in heart distracted
> he brought a double sorrow to fulfillment.
> With patricidal hand
> he reft himself of eyes
> that dearer to him were than his own children.
> And on those children savage
> maledictions he launched
> for their cruel tendance of him
> and wished they might divide
> with iron-wielding hand his own possession.
> And now I fear
> that nimble-footed Fury bring those wishes to fulfillment.
> (Grene's translation, 778–91)

In Aeschylus's *Oedipus* the climax seems to have been the hero's curse on his sons rather than the self-blinding, but the self-blinding implies a new conception of Oedipus's story. Homer's Oedipus, despite suffering, is able to continue as king and even as warrior. Aeschylus's Oedipus is not allowed to continue his life in undiminished power. The incest and parricide arouse a horror and a guilt that drive him to this terrible self-mutilation.

The plague is not mentioned in the myth before Sophocles, and it may well be his invention. It too attaches a strong feeling of horror and pollution to Oedipus's deeds. Incest and parricide, though committed in ignorance, are so deep a violation of the world order that nature responds with sterility and disease. This is a logical development of the Aeschylean view, but it also focuses more sharply on the individual hero. Sophocles may have been influenced as well by the plague that broke out in Athens in 430.

Oedipus's unique intellectual power and his mysterious god-given destiny, enunciated in the oracles, belong to his individual situation as Sophocles conceives it. Blindness and vision, the recognition of ignorance, knowledge, and discovery are also part of Sophocles' distinctive slant on the myth. As in Aeschylus, however, the hero's suffering is not just a personal tragedy; through the crisis in the city and in nature caused by the plague, it is inseparably linked to the political order and the world order.

Although the oracles are important in both Aeschylus and the lyric poet Pindar, Aeschylus's contemporary, Sophocles is the first to make them a leitmotiv of the plot. He is also the first to make the road between Delphi and Thebes the setting for the fatal encounter. Aeschylus, too, used the motif of the ominous triple road, but he located the killing of Laius not on the way to Apollo's oracles at Delphi but at a place called Potniae, south of Thebes, in the direction away from Delphi, where there was a shrine of Demeter and Kore and possibly of the Furies.

The Furies may have had an important role in Aeschylus's *Oedipus*, as they do, for instance, in his *Oresteia*. But he did not invent this part of the myth. The Fury already occurs in Homer's version in the *Odyssey*, as we have seen. About 10 years before Aeschylus's *Seven against Thebes*, Pindar in his *Olympian Odes* alluded to a version that links the oracle and the family curse (*Olympian Odes*, 2.38–42). Sophocles mentioned the family curse in *Antigone*, about 15 years before *Oedipus Tyrannus*. *Oedipus Tyrannus* changes this part of the myth not only by suppressing the old family curse but also by having the hero respond to his discovery of the truth with tenderness and concern for his children, not with a curse (1459ff). Sophocles' change here may even be a deliberate criticism of Aeschylus's work.

Although Sophocles does not neglect the story's divine background (no Greek drama does), he is more interested than is Aeschylus in purely human motivation. Telling the myth in a single play rather than through a trilogy, he cannot trace the continuity of a family curse over three generations as Aeschylus does. He must concentrate on the events in the foreground and can only suggest or hint at the past and the future.

For this reason too Sophocles' treatment of the oracle is very different from Aeschylus's. In Aeschylus's play Laius seems to have received the oracle many years before the birth of Oedipus, and it takes the form of a warning that he must remain childless if he wishes to save his city. But, as Aeschylus's chorus reviews the tale in *Seven against Thebes*, Laius

48

was mastered by loving folly
and begot for himself a doom,
father-murdering Oedipus.
. . . Madness was the coupler
of this distracted pair

                (Grene's translation, 740–57)

Sophocles narrows the temporal perspective of the oracle and also makes it a purely personal matter involving only the father and son. Instead of being a warning, the oracle is an inescapable fact of Laius's life: "His portion will come, to meet death from a son who is born from me and him," is Jocasta's report of the oracle in *Oedipus Tyrannus* (713–14). She repeats this formulation some hundred lines later: "Apollo said that he [Laius] must meet death from his son" (854). When Sophocles has Oedipus defy Teiresias's prophecy of doom with the line, "But if I saved this city I do not care" (443), he may intend a contrast between the civic concern of the son and the foolish and imperious self-centeredness of Aeschylus's Laius.

It is in keeping with Sophocles' interest in character that the oracle makes its first appearance in his play as a feature of Jocasta's skepticism: she wants to prove Delphi's unreliability (711–12). Here too Sophocles focuses on human responses rather than on divine power. But it is noteworthy how little he says about the circumstances in which Laius heard his oracle. Because Laius's oracle in Sophocles does not involve a choice, as it does in Aeschylus, Sophocles can be deliberately vague about these details. With the severe economy that is the hallmark of his art—and of classical art generally—Sophocles restricts the oracle to its most essential effect, driving the parents to put their child out to die. At the same time, Sophocles' use of the oracular motif leaves the role of the gods suggestively and mysteriously in the background.

A chance quotation by an ancient grammarian and a line in Aristophanes enable us to see another Sophoclean innovation, namely the manner of Oedipus's exposure. In Aeschylus, the baby is put out in a terra-cotta pot—at the time a not-uncommon way of practicing this cruel form of population control.[4] Sophocles adds the detail that Laius pierces the feet, presumably to discourage passersby from rescuing the child, and this is the first time that this motif appears in the myth.[5] It brings with it the Herdsman and the Corinthian Messenger, both essential to Sophocles' new focus in the story on the search for a hidden truth about the hero's identity.

The emotional charge that Sophocles gives to the motif of exposing the infant suggests that he may be exploring the guilty feelings that parents would have over the practice. In Euripides' *Ion*, some 20 years later, a mother's self-accusation and remorse last all her life; Oedipus's cry at his discovery also calls attention to what the mother's feelings would have been (1173–75)—a passage that might have more point if women were allowed to attend the dramatic performances. Sophocles, like his contemporary and friend Herodotus in his accounts of infanticide, allows pity for the exposed infant.[6] From the parents' point of view, the oracular commands could reflect the natural anxiety about producing a son with criminal tendencies (in contemporary terms, a sociopath) in a time when rearing any child meant risk and hardship.[7]

OEDIPUS TRAGEDIES IN THE LATE FIFTH CENTURY

Sophocles was not the last tragedian to put the myth of Oedipus on the stage. We know of at least six other plays about Oedipus by fifth-century dramatists; all of them are lost.[8] Euripides wrote an *Oedipus*, probably a dozen or so years after Sophocles, but only fragments survive. He seems to have opened the play with the story of Apollo forbidding Laius to beget a child. He also has Oedipus blinded by the escort of Laius, presumably in punishment for his killing of the king.

In a scene in his comedy *Frogs* (405 B.C.), Aristophanes presents a literary competition between Euripides and Aeschylus in Hades, in which Euripides' *Oedipus* figures prominently. The dramatist quotes the first line of his play, "Oedipus at the outset was a fortunate man," which Aeschylus then criticizes as follows:

> By god, he was not. He was the most *un*fortunate
> from birth. Before birth, since Apollo prophesied
> before he was even begotten, that he would kill his father.
> How could he have been, at the outset, *fortunate*?[9]

Euripides then quotes his second line, "But then he became the wretchedest of humankind." And again Aeschylus offers criticism:

> He didn't *become* the wretchedest. He never stopped.
> Look here. First thing that happened after he was born
> they put him in a broken pot and laid him out in the snow
> so he'd never grow up to be his father's murderer.
> Then he went to Polybus, with swollen feet, wasn't that luck?
> and then he married an old lady, though he was young,
> and also the old lady turned out to be his mother,
> and then he blinded himself . . .

The phrase "with swollen feet" (*oidôn tô pode*) is a pun on the name "Oedipus" and confirms the importance of this kind of wordplay in Sophocles' play. In addition to offering the detail about the exposure in the pot, this passage also shows the popular view of the Oedipus myth as the tale of the greatest possible misfortune.

In one of his last plays, the *Phoenician Women* (ca. 409 B.C.), Euripides returns to the myth of Oedipus, but his main subject, like Aeschylus's *Seven against Thebes*, is the murderous struggle for Thebes by Oedipus's two sons. It is now many years since Oedipus's discovery of the truth and his self-blinding, but Jocasta has not committed suicide, and Oedipus is living in the palace. Jocasta speaks the prologue and summarizes the past. Though basically following the Sophoclean version, Euripides adds some new details. As in Aeschylus, Laius is warned by the oracle not to beget a child or he will destroy both himself and his house; but he yields to "drunkenness and pleasure" and sires Oedipus (*Phoenician Women*, 18–22).

Like Sophocles, Euripides makes father and son meet at the crossroads, but he adds the vivid detail that Laius's horses trample and bloody Oedipus's feet. Thus he follows Sophocles in making the father initiate the aggression, but he replaces Laius's blow at the son's head (807–09) with another wounding of his feet—an act that suggestively repeats Laius's violence against the infant Oedipus. Oedipus then brings Laius's chariot back to Corinth for his supposed father, Polybus (*Phoenician Women*, 42–45). Such examples show how much freedom Greek dramatists could take with the details of a myth and how much they enjoyed adding small variations. Euripides also fills in the details about Laius's oracle that

Sophocles omits. He has Laius consult Delphi because he and Jocasta have been childless for many years (14–16). He is also more precise about how the exposed infant is adopted by King Polybus, adding the detail (possibly borrowed from Herodotus's story of Cyrus the Great) that Polybus's wife passed the baby off as her own.[10]

RIDDLE, KINSHIP, AND LANGUAGE IN THE OEDIPUS MYTH

For Aeschylus and Sophocles the riddle of the Sphinx is a fundamental part of the myth of Oedipus. The earliest reference to the Sphinx, however, is in Hesiod, who describes it as a monster that afflicted Thebes. But in his account its slayer is Heracles, and there is no riddle (*Theogony*, 326–32). The connection of the Sphinx with Oedipus cannot in fact be found any earlier than about 525 B.C., judging from vase paintings. The story of his encounter with the Sphinx seems not to have become popular in Athens before 470–450 B.C. In another version of the story that may also be relatively late (i.e., not much before the fifth century B.C.), Hera sends the Sphinx to punish Thebes for Laius's rape of Chrysippus. It has been argued that the Sphinx is a sixth-century addition to the kernel of the Oedipus myth, perhaps added under Delphic influence, which would emphasize the motifs of oracle, knowledge, and intelligence. Against this view is the new evidence of a black-figure vase from around 520 that not only shows the scene but also gives the text of the riddle in archaic language that suggests the antiquity of both riddle and Sphinx.[11]

   In various versions of the myth, both literary and pictorial, the Sphinx preys on young men, carrying them off in a deadly, quasi-erotic embrace and devouring them. Thus she is a particular danger in the male passage to adulthood. In other tales of this kind, however, the solver of the riddle wins a royal bride and lives happily ever after. By succeeding against the Sphinx Oedipus wins a bride and kingdom, but he also gains bitter unhappiness. Some versions of the story have the defeated Sphinx plunging from a high place to her death, and some interpreters have suggested parallels between this and Jocasta's suicide, viewing the Sphinx, therefore, as a

Oedipus and the Sphinx. Nolan amphora, 450–440 B.C. Bequest
of Mrs. Martin Brimmer. Museum of Fine Arts, Boston.
Photograph courtesy of the Museum of Fine Arts.

Sphinx and Youth (Oedipus?). Attic red-figure lekythos, ca. 460 B.C.
The Art Museum, Princeton University. Gift of Edward Sampson for
the Alden Sampson Collection. *Photograph courtesy of the
Princeton University Art Museum.*

figure for the evil, devouring mother who blocks the son's path to maturity. The word *sphinx* may be related to the Greek verb *sphingein*, to "constrict" or "strangle" (see *sphincter*). The etymology would be appropriate to her function as a demon of death. Little of this aspect of the myth is visible in Sophocles, however, although he does suggest parallels between the supernatural sayings that Oedipus can solve (the Sphinx's riddle) and those that he cannot (Apollo's oracles).

Sophocles' version of the Oedipus story is built in part on a structure of opposites that fuse into one another. He exploits a certain logic encoded into the myth and expressed through the succession of generations. From Oedipus's father, Laius, to his sons, Polyneices and Eteocles, the myth moves from homosexual rape to threatened childlessness and then to incest and the father's deadly curse on his sons. The open prohibition of marital intercourse in Laius's generation leads to too-fertile intercourse in the next generation and then to a surplus of children in the incestuous begetting of two sons who fight for what only one can inherit. Oedipus's marriage contrasts with Laius's (overabundance of children versus threatened childlessness) but is also parallel to it in the transgressive nature of the sexual union it contains: the oracle to Laius prohibiting children is analogous to the oracle to Oedipus foretelling his crime against father and mother that will produce incestuous children.

This is a family whose closeness can only turn inward, against itself. The members are either too close (Oedipus and Jocasta) or too distant (Oedipus and Laius). Indeed the brothers, Polyneices and Eteocles, are both too close and too distant, for each claims his father's heritage within the house, and each treats the other as an enemy in a mutually destructive battle at the gate just outside the city. Laius's line appropriately comes to an end in the third generation when the brothers turn their "excess" of kinship to fratricidal slaughter, which is equivalent to incest in its violation of blood bonds. The two sisters, Antigone and Ismene, behave in a way parallel to the brothers: Antigone commits suicide after her determined attempt to bury one of her fallen brothers in defiance of Creon's decree (the subject of Sophocles' *Antigone*); in other early versions of the myth both Antigone and Ismene are killed. *Antigone* also tells how Creon's son, in love with Antigone, turns against his father in a parricidal gesture that harks back to Oedipus and Laius (*Antigone*, 1231–34), as if contact with Oedipus's house has brought its pattern into Creon's.

The myth offered rich possibilities for exploring the analogies between kinship and language as parallel forms of order and stability that the tragic events of Oedipus's life destroy. Sophocles' use of ambiguous language is both causally and metaphorically related to the confusion of kinship, since Oedipus's multiple generational ties confuse his roles (son and husband to his mother, father and brother to his children); these are a model for linguistic ambiguity in general. Both in its overall pattern and in its specific incidents, Oedipus's life is an anomalous coincidence of progress and regress. This is expressed through the repeated motifs of feet and movement. Instead of passing his father on the road (of life) and letting the older man go on ahead of him (see 800–12), he stopped his father's journey and replaced him, making his own journey forward to a new home, wife, and kingdom coincide with his father's uncompleted journey back to his old home, wife, and kingdom.

The Sphinx, possessing wings, paws, and a human face, is herself a living riddle and so the appropriate figure to stand over the confused locomotion of Oedipus's life. The earliest form of the riddle that comes down to us uses feet to ask about the different generations of mankind: "There is on earth a being two-footed, four-footed, and three-footed that has one name [literally, one voice]; and, of all creatures that move upon earth and in the heavens and in the sea, it alone changes its form. But when it goes propped on most feet, then is the swiftness in its limbs the weakest."[12] The riddle points to the precarious, changing nature of man: of all creatures he alone uses his intelligence to change his mode of locomotion as he progresses through life. As the very existence of the riddle implies, he alone is conscious of his uniqueness in nature. Oedipus, as self-aware, intelligent Man, is the solver of his own riddle. Indeed his name, in one possible etymology, suggests the meaning "Know Foot" (*oida*, "I know," and *pous*, "foot")—that is, "He who knows the riddle of the feet."

The riddle also combines man's power and weakness and so points to Oedipus in a very different sense because he is the most contradictory of men in his combination of intelligence and ignorance. His essence, therefore, is even more unstable than the shifting identity of generic "man." He can answer the riddle because he is its hidden subject. Indeed, the Sphinx's word for "two-footed," *dipous*, the riddle's first item, evokes the name of 'Oe-*dipous*. But even his two-footedness is precarious, for he walks through life on the pierced feet that were "yoked" together in order to prevent him from walking at all, and he struck his father down with the staff that is his "third foot" (see 810–12).

Only Sophocles presents his hero struggling with riddles, and these are essential to the Sophoclean interpretation of the myth. Oedipus both answers and acts out the riddle's answer, for he is himself the quintessence of the being to whom the riddle points. The answer to the riddle is both "Man" and "Oedipus." Oedipus gives the first answer to the Sphinx in the events before the play begins, and he gives the second answer to us, the audience, within the play. But of course both answers are intertwined, as Oedipus is Sophocles' model of Tragic Man. It is his—and man's—fundamental nature always to be a riddle to himself and never to be reducible to a single, sure meaning. Hence the riddlelike ambiguities of language in the play are not just a surface effect of Sophocles' poetry; they are also an expression of the tragic meaning. Sophocles' genius lay in his ability to crystalize the myth's tragic paradoxes in the ambiguities and ironies of his language and plot and to interweave these ironies so richly with the issues of knowledge and self-discovery, illusion and reality, the meaning or nonsense of life.

SOME MODERN INTERPRETATIONS OF THE OEDIPUS MYTH

The systematic study of myth in the nineteenth century brought a number of interpretations to the Oedipus myth, including the famous interpretation by Sigmund Freud, which we shall presently discuss. Only some of the nineteenth-century readings are relevant to Sophocles' play. Interpreters do not always distinguish clearly between the play and the myth as it occurs outside the play. This distinction becomes even harder to make because we must recognize that the Oedipus myth today is to some extent a modern construct produced by synthesizing and analyzing the total narrative pattern that emerges when we put all the variants together.

Sophocles' three Oedipus plays have become *sources* for the myth as well as *versions* and even *interpretations* of the myth. Additionally, in a living oral culture like that of early Greece a given myth has many possible forms: it is a configuration of narrative elements that lends itself to a different selection and elaboration of details each time it is told. For these reasons, it is probably futile to try to reconstruct the "original myth." These considerations have not stopped scholars from speculating, however—a harmless enough activity, as long as one is clear about whether the *play* or the *myth* (or both) is the subject of speculation.

Hegel, the nineteenth-century German philosopher, approached the myth in terms of the development of human consciousness and saw in the figure of Oedipus Western man's dawning moral and intellectual self-awareness. Oedipus shows the emergence of an ethical sense and an acknowledgment of guilt after the lack of consciousness of committing a crime.[13] Friedrich Nietzsche viewed Oedipus as the paradigm of man's guilt about his power to dominate nature. To solve the riddle of the Sphinx is to solve "the riddle of nature," he said. The "unnatural acts" of incest and parricide show wisdom itself as an "unnatural crime" through which man does violence to nature, forcing it to "yield up her secrets."[14]

At the opposite extreme from these rather general, symbolic interpretations are historical views, like that of H. J. Rose, who found in the myth the kernel of historical kings in Mycenaean Thebes. The Russian folklorist Vladimir Propp suggested that the myth reflects the transition between a matrilinear and a patrilinear mode of succession. It develops, he argues, at a point of historical change from inheriting the kingship through the mother to gaining it through the father. The killing of a king by the husband of his daughter is a common folklore motif. In stories of the Oedipus type, however, the son, not the son-in-law, is the subject of dangerous omens and prophecies and the one who is feared as the old king's killer.[15]

Looking to an even more remote past, some have seen in Oedipus the remnants of an ancient fertility god or a pattern of sacred kingship, of the type familiar from Sir James Frazer's vast survey of myth and ritual, *The Golden Bough*, wherein the old king has to be killed and replaced by a younger and more potent successor.[16] Others have brought Oedipus closer to earth as a figure of folklore—stressing the affinities with folklore motifs like the riddle and the transparently significant name—but recast into a moralized form by a patriarchal society that stigmatizes crimes against the father as the worst of all possible deeds.[17]

The most influential reading of the myth and the play in our century has come not from classical studies or myth criticism but from psychology, from the work of Sigmund Freud, founder of psychoanalysis. The play fascinates us so much, Freud suggested, not because it dramatizes "the contrast between destiny and human will," but because "there must be something which makes a voice within us ready to recognize the compelling force of destiny."[18] This "destiny" is the universal necessity to which all of us (or at least all males) are subject—namely, the wishes that remain from our buried animal nature to kill the father and possess the mother.

For Freud, the oracle that Oedipus receives about his life from Apollo contains the repressed wishes of the unconscious. Because we cannot escape having these wishes, deny them though we will, they constitute our secret destiny. Freud set forth his view of Oedipus succinctly in *The Interpretation of Dreams*:

> His destiny moves us only because it might have been ours—because the oracle laid the same curse upon us before our birth as upon him. It is the fate of all of us, perhaps, to direct our first sexual impulse towards our mother and our first hatred and our first murderous wish against our father. Our dreams convince us that this is so. King Oedipus, who slew his Father Laius and married his mother Jocasta, merely shows us the fulfilment of our own childhood wishes. . . . Here is one in whom these primaeval wishes of our childhood have been fulfilled, and we shrink back from him with the whole force of the repression by which those wishes have since that time been held down within us. (Freud, 296)

Freud continued to reflect on the play throughout his life and to refine his interpretations. In his late essay "Dostoevsky and Parricide" he suggests that the external objectification of Oedipus's crime in the oracle is a way of "projecting the hero's unconscious motive into reality in the form of a compulsion by a destiny which is alien to him."[19] And in one of his last works he speculates that this disguising of Oedipus's unconscious desires in the form of an oracle from the gods not only lets the unconscious become visible but also accounts for the feeling of guilt that we have about these unconscious desires, even though we are not guilty of any crime. He paraphrases the play as telling the viewer, "In vain do you deny that you are accountable, in vain do you proclaim how you have striven against these evil designs. You are guilty, nevertheless; for you could not stifle them; they still survive unconsciously in you."[20]

Freud addressed the issue of guilt in a slightly different way in his essay on Dostoevsky, in which he suggested that Oedipus's eagerness to punish himself, with no attempt at self-defense, corresponds to the inner conviction of guilt that stems from these unconscious desires: "the hero makes no attempt to exculpate himself by appealing to the artificial expedient of the compulsion of destiny. His crime is acknowledged and punished as though it were fully conscious—which is bound to appear unjust to our reason, but which psychologically is perfectly correct."[21]

The central role of Sophocles' Oedipus as a model for the unconscious, in Freud's thinking, led Freud to give the name "Oedipus complex" to a major tenet of psychoanalytic theory. The Oedipus complex denotes each person's attitudes and behavior in his or her most intimate family relationships, especially to mother and father. To mature as an emotionally healthy, non-neurotic adult, the child, according to Freud, must somehow come to terms with the residue of repressed infantile hatred and desire for his or her parents.

The mixture of primordial, hidden desires and aggressions that belong to the Oedipus complex, and the guilt that derives from living with them in the unconscious, are, in Freud's view, what create the sexual dynamics of the personality. This view, however, has been increasingly questioned and modified in recent years. Critics of Freud's theories have objected to his rather mechanistic and deterministic approach to human behavior, his extreme concentration on sexuality and sexual repression, his neglect of gender differences and of the role of culture in forming the human personality, his tendency to universalize factors that may belong to a specific historical moment, and his lack of close attention to the pre-verbal and pre-oedipal stages of the child's life, the first two or three years. On the other hand, the widespread popularity of tales of the Oedipus type throughout many parts of the world does lend support to the basic validity of Freud's theories.

While Freud's Oedipus complex may now seem to be a rather limited way of understanding Sophocles' play, there is more promising material in his sensitive remarks on the *process* of discovering unconscious knowledge enacted in *Oedipus Tyrannus*. In *The Interpretation of Dreams* Freud observes, "The action of the play consists in nothing other than the process of revealing, with cunning delays and ever-mounting excitement—a process that can be likened to the work of a psychoanalysis—that Oedipus himself is the murderer of Laius, but further that he is the son of the murdered man and of Jocasta" (Freud, 295). Whether or not Freud's theories about infantile fantasies stand the test of time, there is profound truth in his insight about the way in which *Oedipus Tyrannus* takes its audience through a deeply involving process of uncovering hidden truths about the self. It was an important insight to relate this process to the uncovering of the unconscious, whatever the exact contents of the unconscious may be.

In dramatizing the discovery of a hidden truth about oneself, the play may be said to anticipate the model of psychoanalysis. Its powerful effect, Freud once suggested, lies in the viewer's reacting "as though by self-analysis he had detected the Oedipus complex in himself and had recognized the will of the gods as glorified disguises of his own unconscious."[22] But the opposite is also true: psychoanalysis is a systematic technique for reaching the kind of knowledge that the play can bring to a fully involved spectator. Analytical and descriptive language (like mine in this book) can attempt to re-create or account for this experience after the fact but cannot reproduce the living power of the effect itself. As Freud once observed, the unconscious was discovered long before psychoanalysis; Freud was merely the first to give it a name. Both Sophocles and Freud are concerned with forcing into conscious speech and, in the case of *Oedipus Tyrannus*, into clear, theatrical vision knowledge that has been repressed into the darkness of the unknowable and unspeakable.

It is important to confront honestly and undogmatically the limitations of a Freudian analysis of classical (and other) literature. A Freudian reading is unhistorical in character, inattentive to esthetic form, and disregards cultural differences. Freudian interpretation runs the risk of merely interposing a text from contemporary culture between ourselves and antiquity. Freud's surest contribution to literary study, however, lies in his conception of the unconscious: a realm of primordial desires, fears, and impulses that the censorship of our conscious mind allows to appear only through the distorting mechanisms of symbol making, condensation, displacement, splitting, and the like, that clothe the contents of the unconscious in forms acceptable to our conscious minds.

A Freudian reading illuminates *Oedipus Tyrannus* because it points to the central theme of concealing and revealing terrible knowledge. It may be said that Oedipus's passion for knowledge, his determination to discover his past, is at least as strong as his blindness to the clues in his path, but the tragic situation and its ironies lie precisely in this discrepancy between the will to know and the long persistence in ignorance.

The Freudian critic operates with the hypothesis that the subject refuses to know what he (unconsciously) knows and, furthermore, that this process of paradoxical knowledge-in-ignorance is enacted in language.[23] Thus Oedipus not only refuses to "hear" the truth that Teiresias plainly speaks to him but repeatedly gives details about himself that he does not recognize as truth. In the prologue, for example, he seems to say, by a typical "Freudian slip" of the tongue, that a single robber, not "many robbers," killed Laius (124). Later, with the same "innocence," he offers to fight for Laius as if "for my own father," since he and Laius, as he says, possess a "wife of common seeding" and children "in common" (260ff). This inability to acknowledge the truths about himself that his own language utters exemplifies the resistance to knowing consciously what lies buried in his unconscious.

One could go even further and suggest that Oedipus has defended himself against his incestuous and parricidal wishes by splitting each mother figure and father figure into two—the consciously acknowledged parents at Corinth, Merope and Polybus, from whom he must be separated forever by the oracle's prohibition against incest and parricide, and the unacknowledged parents at Thebes, against whom he unknowingly commits just these crimes. Our pleasure in the irony for which the play is famous lies in the shiver of excitement and recognition that we feel when the unconscious tries to surface to the conscious mind—that is, when we can see acted out in language before us the usually invisible processes of denying unconscious knowledge. This is the effect that Freud described as "the uncanny." Indirectly, Freud's reading of *Oedipus Tyrannus* suggests how a literary work uses the processes of disguise, gradual revelation, and symbolism to make us experience areas and forms of knowledge to which we can have access in no other way.[24]

There is, however, a major difference between the Sophoclean and the Freudian irrational. For Sophocles, the irrational lies outside as well as within. It is embodied in the gods, in the mysterious ways of Apollo, and in the gods' messages to men: the oracles and the plague. For Freud, the irrational is our "fate" or destiny in the sense that it is built in to our emotional makeup, as it is evolved with the development of human civilization. For Sophocles, the surd, the irrational, really is an *other*, an aspect of the divine outside of and apart from man. For Freud this *other* is projected inwardly, as a part of our own mind, something hidden within ourselves.

AFTER FREUD: THREE CONTEMPORARY INTERPRETATIONS

The contradictions surrounding the figure of Oedipus continue to fascinate students of the play and the myth, and I shall discuss here three influential recent interpreters, all French: Claude Lévi-Strauss, the founder of structural anthropology, the classicist Jean-Pierre Vernant, and the literary and cultural critic René Girard.

Lévi-Strauss views the myth in terms of a mediation of opposites—that is, the mind's attempt to make sense of the world by finding a middle term that reconciles fundamental contradictions, like life and death.[25] The myth consists of all of its versions taken together simultaneously, from Laius to Antigone's death, in *synchronic* order, not just in sequential (diachronic) order. This mode of reading reveals an underlying structure that has to do with the balance between underrating and overrating kin relations. Killing one's father, for example, is an undervaluation of kin ties;

Antigone's insistence on burying her brother at the cost of her own life is an overvaluation.

For Lévi-Strauss, incest and parricide are not the real subject of the myth. They are only elements in a larger signifying system, a "code," which can be understood only in relation to other elements in the system. The extremes of overvaluing or undervaluing kin ties express logical contradictions and their mediation. Tracing the house of Oedipus back to its founder, Cadmus, Lévi-Strauss sees the successive generations as alternating between the overvaluation and undervaluation of kin ties. He finds another constant in the themes of walking and lameness in the family of Oedipus, and he imaginatively decodes this motif of lameness as pointing to autochthony (being born from the earth). This combination of elements is the clue to the logic or "structure" underlying the myth: it provides a model for reconciling the primordial belief that humankind is sprung from the earth (i.e., born from only "one") with the knowledge that humans are born from the sexual union of a man and a woman (that is, from "two"). To make sense of our human identity, in other words, we have to reconcile the conflicting propositions, "born from different, born from same"; or, in Freudian terms, we have to understand "how *one* can be born from *two*."

Many critics have rejected Lévi-Strauss's focus on autochthony as arbitrary, and this motif is probably less applicable to Sophocles' version of the myth than to Aeschylus's.[26] Still, his essay is a bold and pioneering attempt to read the myth in terms of its underlying logic of simultaneously coexisting opposites. The logic of "same" versus "other" is certainly relevant to other parts of the myth, although not necessarily in the terms set out by Lévi-Strauss. It may, for example, apply to the ambivalence between the hero's conflict with the father and his reenacting the role of the father—being *other* than the father or being the *same* as the father by repeating his pattern of violence and aggression.

Jean-Pierre Vernant also reads the myth in terms of an underlying logic of paradox, but he grounds his approach in a more historical situation.[27] Oedipus's position as the ruler and the perpetrator of incest belongs to the model of excessive behavior often attributed to "tyrants" in early history, like the sixth-century tyrant Periander in Herodotus (*Histories*, 5.92). Indeed, Plato, in the next century, in his discussion of the deformed soul of the tyrant at the beginning of book 9 of the *Republic*, combines incest and unrestrained appetite as features of the tyrant's lawlessness and bestiality (*Republic*, 9.571cff). The pattern appears in the mythicized accounts of Roman history's most infamous tyrants: Tarquin's rape of Lucretia (Livy, *Histories*, 1.58–59) and the emperor Nero's alleged incest with his mother, Agrippina (Suetonius, *Life of Nero*, chap. 28).

Oedipus's movement from high to low, Vernant suggests, also parallels the ancient Greek institution of the scapegoat, or *pharmakos* (Vernant, 97–111). In a ceremony that was still performed in Sophocles' day, two scapegoats—people symbolically laden with all the troubles and pollutions of the community—were driven through the town and then ritually expelled (originally they may have been stoned to death). Sophocles' Oedipus is not, of course, literally expelled, but he wants to be, and in any case he gives up his kingship. In Vernant's structure of reversals, the plague creates a situation in which the people are ready to sacrifice their king as a scapegoat. This is in fact almost the situation in Voltaire's adaptation of the play. By bringing king and scapegoat together in a single person, Oedipus reveals the scapegoat as "the king's double, but reversed like the carnival kings crowned for the duration of the festival, when order is turned upside down and the social hierarchies reversed: . . . and in these circumstances the one who sits upon the throne must be the lowest, the most ugly, the most ridiculous, the most criminal" (Vernant, 104).

Vernant makes a further connection between the expulsion of the once-powerful king and the Athenian democracy's institution of ostracism, begun in the early years of the fifth century. In the system of ostracism the people voted on which one of a select number of powerful leaders should go into exile. The system was devised to avert a political crisis that could result in civil war or the usurpation of power by a tyrant (in the word's original sense, as one who gained power by force rather than by election or inheritance). Oedipus, then, simultaneously the highest and the lowest in the city, is both the leader who accepts ostracism and the scapegoat who bears all that is ugliest and most harmful.

For René Girard, in his *Violence and the Sacred*, the central issue is the control of violence.[28] Tragedy forces society to recognize the violence that lies at its center. The Oedipus myth, Girard says, shows all masculine relations as "based on reciprocal acts of violence" (Girard, 48). Laius's violence against his son is perpetuated in the son's against the father. The cultural distinction between "father" and "son" is destroyed, and the plague that follows is an expression of this disease of random violence. Order is restored by the unanimous selection and expulsion of a scapegoat, which enables the community to reunite and thus escape from its endless cycle of revenge and retribution.

According to Girard, the plague parallels the parricide and the incest as the sign of an infectious violence that results from the destruction of differences. The action consists in a desperate hunt for a scapegoat, a sacrificial victim (Girard, 78). With the identification of Oedipus as the criminal, the crisis can be resolved and the violence now directed toward its proper victim, not randomly against the victims of the plague. By thus giving violence back to the gods, making it sacred and taboo once more, the society can restore its lost sense of differentiation and order.

Girard's stimulating essay is valuable for its recognition of the collapse of differences as the focus of the crisis depicted in the play and of the importance in the myth of the equivalence between Laius and Oedipus in their respective aggressive acts. Yet Sophocles' text (unlike the later versions by Corneille and Voltaire) does not place much emphasis on the mechanism of sacrifice, and Girard's theory works less well for this play than for such others as Euripides' *Bacchae*. His emphasis on the arbitrariness in the selection of the scapegoat and on the victim's submission also dissolves the concern with personal responsibility and justice that are important in both the play and the myth. Although Girard makes a valid attempt to find a mythic structure concealed by the moral interpretation of the play, one cannot help suspecting that he superimposes his own reading on the mythical material: "From the purely religious point of view, the surrogate victim—or more simply, the final victim—inevitably appears as a being who submits to violence without provoking a reprisal; a supernatural being who sows violence to reap peace; a mysterious savior who visits affliction on mankind in order subsequently to restore it to good health" (Girard, 86). Girard's savior-victim here is more like Christ in the Gospels than Oedipus.

CURSES AND BLESSINGS

The myth of Oedipus, like many Greek myths, is concerned with the mystery and danger of power. The hero is the conduit of powerful energies of creation and destruction, and he brings these into his city as a result of his special closeness to the gods. More exposed than other men and women to such numinous power, the hero can reach the highest or lowest points on the scale of human values. Not only in Sophocles' play but also in related mythical patterns the hero of the Oedipus type becomes both a wondrous savior and a wicked criminal. In medieval legend the Oedipal pattern—oracle, exposure in infancy, killing the father, and marrying the mother—applies to the diametrically opposite figures, Judas and Saint (later Pope) Gregory. In the one set of legends the "Oedipus figure" becomes the most accursed of men, Judas Iscariot, who betrays Christ and finally hangs himself in despair. In the other set he attains the highest sanctity: Saint Gregory, on discovering the truth of his incestuous marriage, is overwhelmed by guilt and has a fisherman lock him up in a cellar where he lives in solitary penance, is miraculously found, and named pope.[29]

Oedipus at Colonus, which Sophocles wrote in the last years of his life, shows how the coincidence of accursed outcast and holy man already existed in the paradoxes surrounding the ancient hero. Oedipus is now an old, blind exile and wanderer. Sustained through years of misery by his faithful daughter Antigone, he eventually arrives at Athens. He knows of a mysterious oracle that his bones will protect whatever city receives him for burial. But Creon, now king of Thebes, also knows this oracle and tries to seize Oedipus and bring him back to his old city by force. Oedipus refuses, and Theseus, king of Athens, protects him. The play ends with the gods suddenly calling Oedipus to his resting place. Henceforth his body, from its tomb known only to Theseus, will protect Athens from foreign invaders. Despite the blessings that the old Oedipus will bring to his adoptive city, however, he still arouses awe and horror in those who met him, and he still curses, angrily and bitterly, the sons who drove him out. For all his special gifts from the gods, he is not saintly in the Christian sense—like Gregory. He remains a dangerous and violent figure, the source of maledictions as well as of blessings.

The ambiguity that continues to surround Oedipus is marked in the transgressive act that opens *Oedipus at Colonus*: he reenacts the danger of his special relation to divinity by entering a heavily tabooed grove sacred to the dread Eumenides. These goddesses are a somewhat gentler form of the Furies, but they are still awesome powers, the daughters of Earth and Darkness. The play takes its name from the setting of this grove, at the edge of Athens, near the Athenian locale of Colonus, where Oedipus is also to be buried. In Sophocles' time he was worshiped there as a local divinity.

In entering this shrine and steadfastly refusing to leave, Oedipus is in a way reenacting his initial crime, trespassing in a sacred female space forbidden to him. As in the earlier phase of his life, he is again the stranger and intruder who claims a place in a foreign city. To find his way into this new home, he must also pass through trials, as he did at his first arrival at Thebes in his youth (see Chapter 6). But his entrance into Athens also contrasts with that earlier entrance into Thebes, because at Athens he resolves his ambiguous status as both insider and outsider.

Athens often functions in classical tragedy as the place for the recovery and reintegration of a conflicted personality and for the successful resolution of familial conflict, whereas Thebes (as we also see in *Seven against Thebes*, *Antigone*, and *Bacchae*) is the place for disastrous confusions of identity and unresolved family conflicts.[30] Thus at Thebes, in *Oedipus Tyrannus*, Oedipus is pulled back into his family's self-destructive, accursed past and can only repeat it, even though he is under the illusion that he is finding a new identity. At Athens, in *Oedipus at Colonus*, he begins with full clarity about the relations of past and present, wanderer and citizen, weakness and strength, and he escapes all the attempts to drag him back to Thebes.

Oedipus's apparent trespass into the Eumenides' grove at the beginning of *Oedipus at Colonus*, then, proves to be part of a divinely sanctioned plan to give him rest, not to force him out of an illusionary security. Whereas the remote gods of *Oedipus Tyrannus* reveal his terrible "sickness" of pollution beneath an apparent power to cure, now they reveal the feeble, battered body as a source of mysterious power. Oedipus is still a living contradiction. What is more paradoxical than a miserable, blind beggar who can defend a city from powerful armies? The terms are almost exactly the reverse of those in *Oedipus Tyrannus*.

Despite the two plays' differences, the later shares the earlier's pattern of the hero who combines the extremes of power and weakness. *Oedipus at Colonus*, however, reinterprets the pattern from the perspective of the end rather than the beginning of Oedipus's life. Where *Oedipus Tyrannus* traces the process of uncovering a hidden past, *Oedipus Colonus* begins with a hero who already holds the secrets of his life's beginning and end, has a privileged knowledge of his contact with divinity, and is fully aware of his special power for the future.

6

Oedipus and the Trials
of the Hero

THE MYTH OF THE HERO

Viewed in its simplest form, the Oedipus myth is a version of the myth of the hero. It resembles the stories of Perseus, Jason, Theseus, Cyrus the Great, Moses, Romulus and Remus, Siegfried, and many others. Persecuted by a hostile father or father figure (uncle, grandfather, king), because of a warning or omens at or before his birth, the hero is threatened with death as an infant—left to die in the woods, or set adrift in a sea or river. In some myths the real father is a god; in others, the child is born of incest. Rescued from death and raised by foreign parents or sometimes by animals, he gives signs in his youth of remarkable powers. When he grows up, he performs great deeds, often killing monsters (as did Theseus, Perseus, Jason, and Oedipus). Through his prowess he regains his kingdom, wins a bride, punishes the evil father figure, and discovers and restores his lost parents.

As Sophocles presents him in *Oedipus Tyrannus*, however, Oedipus enacts the hero myth in reverse. Whereas the other heroes are confirmed in their adult status and power when they discover their true birth, Oedipus's move back to his infancy is disastrous. Sophocles' hero calls on the place where he was left to die as an infant, Mount Cithaeron (1391–93, 1451–54). In other hero myths the protagonist proves to be the son of a god; in *Oedipus Tyrannus* the chorus *hopes* that Oedipus will prove to be the son of a god

(1098–1109) but immediately afterwards discovers the opposite, that Oedipus is the land's pollution.

The Sphinx corresponds to the dragon or monster in other myths of the hero: the dragon that guards the golden fleece in the Jason myth; the dragon that guards the accursed gold in the tale of Siegfried; the sea serpent and the Chimaera in the myths of Perseus and Bellerophon, respectively. The Sphinx seems, in fact, to combine the "princess who sets the task" with the "dragon who demands tribute in human blood" in the familiar tales of the fairy-tale hero.[1] But in the Oedipus myth the Sphinx always appears in high places—on a hill, mountain, or column, never in a cave—and Oedipus combats it by solving a riddle, not by using a sword or spear. The few vases that do show martial combat probably represent a later, secondary development, following the more common type of hero myth.[2]

TRIALS OF THE HERO

As a series of trials characteristic of the myth of the hero, the story of Oedipus has the following form. (1) The young man is challenged about his birth and (2) goes on a journey to discover his true origins. (3) He makes inquiry of a god and (4) receives a mysterious answer. (5) Instead of returning home, he continues his journey into a strange land, where (6) he meets his first challenge, an older, regal figure who stands in his way, blocking his road. The encounter with this blocking figure is his first heroic combat (7), and he defeats and kills his opponent. He then meets a second trial on his path, the Sphinx (8), whom he also defeats and kills, thereby (9) winning the queen and (10) gaining the throne.

Sophocles has made this hero myth one of tragedy instead of triumph by making the prophecy (no. 4) a terrible one and by combining the meeting with the father (no. 7) with the meeting with the Sphinx (no. 8) into a composite first trial. Recast into its tragic mode, the myth is dominated by anxiety, uncertainty, lack of control, and the problem of self-knowledge. In the life crisis dramatized in *Oedipus Tyrannus*, the hero can move forward only by reaching backward to the past. And so Sophocles' plot unfolds as the recovery of lost knowledge and a lost past.

As an inverted form of the hero myth, Oedipus's success at each stage really hides a terrible failure. His strengths are eventually revealed as sources of defeat and weakness, culminating in his self-blinding. This pattern is replicated in Oedipus's trials within the play, of which the first is the plague. Both the priest in the opening scene and the chorus in the first ode describe its devastations. Even before the midpoint of the action, however, it is simply forgotten. Oedipus's search for his origins completely overshadows the sufferings of the city that have set the plot into motion. We hear of the plague for the last time when Jocasta reproaches Oedipus and Creon for quarreling in private while "the land suffers from such a disease" (635f).

The hero's trials that follow from the plague take the form of a series of personal encounters. These are almost juridical inquiries, and they fall into two groups of three meetings each. All six show Oedipus's keen intelligence in action as he tries to solve the murder of Laius and the mystery of the plague by careful cross-examination, often in line-by-line exchange.

The first three tests are, respectively, Oedipus's meetings with Creon, Teiresias, and then Creon again. In each case he is pursuing the killer as someone whom he assumes is *other* than himself (87–131, 316–462, 513–630). The second series begins with Jocasta and continues with the Corinthian Messenger and Laius's Herdsman. Now Oedipus is pursuing the killer as possibly the *same* as himself (726–862, 954–1085, 1119–85). In this set his goal shifts gradually from uncovering the murderer to discovering his own parents. The confidence and power that he demonstrated in the first series of encounters gradually erode into anger, loss of control, and fear.

This second series of tests comes not in personal encounters with men onstage but from the remote past and from the gods. Oedipus swings between fear and hope as he encounters unknown figures from his past, first the Messenger and then Laius's Herdsman. Oedipus will now have to make the final decision, whether to cross the hairline from uncertainty to certain knowledge (1169–70). By introducing this hesitation at the moment of discovery, Sophocles makes the truth emerge as a deliberate act of will: Oedipus takes on himself the decision to cross the divide that will henceforth separate him from all men.

After this climactic moment, Oedipus's encounters belong to a more private realm and are dominated by emotion rather than intellectual inquiry. Instead of a king addressing subjects in the civic space outside the palace, he rushes within, to find Jocasta already dead by her own hand in the most intimate chamber of the palace. Whereas the previous meetings have consisted of dialogue and argument, this one, which we learn of only through the report of the Messenger, consists of the violent act of the self-blinding.

How will Oedipus confront the world after these discoveries and these sufferings? The remainder of the play pursues this question and completes the hero's trials. Again there is a series of three meetings, each a test of the new non–King Oedipus. First he encounters the chorus of his citizen-subjects, then Creon, and finally his two young daughters, Antigone and Ismene. Like the first series of tests, these three encounters move from Oedipus's public to his personal life, but now they try his courage, endurance, and capacity for learning through suffering, rather than his intelligence or competence.

Oedipus's strength of spirit determines the quality of the play's final test, his last meeting with Creon. Oedipus is troubled and embarrassed as the chorus announces the approach of the man whom Oedipus had almost condemned to death for his own crime (1419–21). Creon's pity and moderation make Oedipus's situation easier, but then the mood of the scene shifts surprisingly. Oedipus turns from his utter desolation and abasement to something of his old air of command, albeit in a chastened and softened tone. He asks Creon to expel him from Thebes as quickly as he can and gives orders for Jocasta's burial (1446ff), a gesture of concern and responsibility characteristic of the Oedipus we saw in the opening scenes. The conflict of authority with Creon changes to a gentler, more personal, and more intimate tone as Creon, anticipating Oedipus's wish, brings him his daughters.

Crosscurrents of anger and conflict between Oedipus and Creon still threaten the stability of the last scene in a way reminiscent of Achilles' precarious self-control before Priam in *Iliad*. For a moment Oedipus vacillates between his old, hasty imperiousness and his present acceptance of helplessness, between wanting expulsion from his human community and wanting closeness to his family. This is a test of Oedipus very different from that of the opening scene. Creon, too, keeps a delicate balance, between generosity and rebuke.

The entire action of the play may be viewed as one huge, collective test, a reenactment of Oedipus's contest with the Sphinx. In the course of the play the intellectual power that made possible his external victory over the monster is increasingly directed to the harder riddles of his own origins and the horrible secrets of his life. The result seems to be defeat rather than victory—or is it defeat after all? Oedipus does succeed: he solves the riddle of who he is, and he has the strength to endure the suffering that he has found: "No man but I can bear my evil doom" (1415). The Oedipus who emerges from this final trial is more like a prophet than a king. He has lost his eyes but gained something of Teiresias's vision of truth.

The chorus had introduced Teiresias as the only man who had truth "inborn, as part of his nature" (299). Having become blind, like Teiresias, to gain a new kind of sight, Oedipus will now live a life of truth rather than illusion. But his truth is gained through painful effort, not given as an inborn quality like the truth that Teiresias possesses (299). What Oedipus was "born" with leads him into darkness, illusion, and deception. After confronting this truth Oedipus finds his trials coming from within rather than from the outside, and here the issue is neither victory nor defeat, only understanding and endurance.

7

Life's Tragic Shape:
Plot, Design, Destiny

One of the hardest problems in approaching *Oedipus Tyrannus* is trying to look at it freshly. To do that, one must remove a few layers of misconception; so I have to begin with a few "nots." This is *not* a play about free will versus determinism. The Greeks did not develop a notion of a universal, all-determining fate before the third century B.C. The human characters are not mere puppets of the gods; no figure in Greek tragedy is. To be sure, the supernatural elements are important: Apollo, the plague, the oracles, Teiresias's prophetic knowledge. But the play does not label any of these as the certain *causes* of suffering. There are no gods onstage, as happens regularly in Aeschylus and Euripides. For all its concern with prophecy and oracles, *Oedipus Tyrannus* has a startling modernity precisely because these supernatural elements are not only kept in the background but are also hidden and mysterious.

The issues of destiny, predetermination, and foreknowledge are raised as problems, *not* as dogma. How much control do we have over the shape of our lives? How much of what happens to us is due to heredity, to accidents, to sheer luck (good and bad), to personality, to the right (or wrong) decision at a particular crossroads in life, or to the myriad interactions among all of the above? These are the questions that the play raises, and it raises them *as questions*. It shows us men and women who are both powerful and

75

helpless, often at the same moment. Oedipus embodies the human condition in just this paradoxical relation to both open and closed conceptions of life. He is both free and determined, both able to choose and helpless in the face of choices that he has already made in the past or circumstances (like those of his birth) over which he had no power of choice. The play, as one interpreter remarks, shows us the issues of choice and predetermination as "a box of mirrors to bewilder each new generation; the whole tangle is here in this story. . . . The play offers to each spectator as much as he is capable of seeing."[1]

Although it is customary to group Antigone, Oedipus Tyrannus, and Oedipus at Colonus together as the three Theban plays because they deal with the royal house of Thebes, the three works were not conceived as a trilogy. Antigone was written more than a decade before Oedipus Tyrannus, and Oedipus at Colonus was composed some 20 years after. There are numerous verbal echoes of Antigone in Oedipus Tyrannus and of both plays in Oedipus at Colonus, which self-consciously looks back to these two works. It is helpful, therefore, to have the earlier works in mind when reading the later ones, but esthetically the three works are independent.

Oedipus does not have a tragic flaw. This view rests on a misreading of Aristotle and is a moralizing way out of the disturbing questions that the play means to ask. Sophocles refuses to give so easy an answer to the problem of suffering. Oedipus's haste and irascibility at crucial moments (particularly in the killing of Laius) contribute to the calamity but are not sufficient reasons for it nor its main cause.

Finally, the play does not end with the self-blinding of Oedipus, but in fact goes on for another 300 lines. These closing scenes are essential for understanding how Sophocles conceives of his hero and should not be neglected.

The tragic effect of Oedipus Tyrannus lies in part in its dramatic irony, long ago observed by Aristotle: what seems to be bringing salvation in fact brings destruction. In the first scene the Theban priest invokes Oedipus as the "savior" from the plague, when in fact he is its cause. Later Oedipus will curse the man who was his savior from death when he was exposed on the mountain in infancy (1349–54). Despite all the attempts to avoid the three oracles—the oracles to Laius in the remote past, to Oedipus some 20 years ago at Delphi, and to Thebes in the present—they all come true.

The plot that unfolds this situation may look like a diabolical trap set for Oedipus by the gods (which is the direction Jean Cocteau's reworking of the play, *The Infernal Machine*, follows), but Sophocles lets us see these events as the natural result of an interaction between character, circumstances in the past, and mere chance combinations in the present. Nevertheless, by placing the oracles in so prominent a position in the action, Sophocles from the first scene makes the question of divine intervention unavoidable. The play forces us to ask where the gods are in this tale of extraordinary coincidences and extraordinary suffering. Even the supernatural element of the oracles operates in a human way.

Typically in Greek tragedy the gods work through normal human behavior and motivation. They are, one might say, an added dimension of our reality, not an arbitrary negation of reality. What we mean by calling *Oedipus Tyrannus* a tragedy of fate might be more accurately phrased as Sophocles' sense of the existence of powers working in the world in ways alien to and hidden from human understanding. Karl Reinhardt has put the ancient view very well: "For Sophocles, as for the Greeks of an earlier age, fate is in no circumstances the same as predetermination, but is a spontaneous unfolding of daimonic power."[2] The play leaves it an open question whether Laius, Jocasta, or Oedipus might have prevented the fulfillment of the prophecies if they had simply done nothing: not exposed the infant, not consulted Delphi, not avoided Thebes, not married an older woman, and so on.

In contrast to Aeschylus, as we have seen, Sophocles' oracles do not give commands or advice; they simply state the way things are. How things got that way we do not know: this is part of the mystery that surrounds the tragic shape they have. All we can say, and all the play shows us, is that the events do work out as the god said they would and that the human figures bring about these events through a chain of actions that contains some striking coincidences but is nevertheless within the realm of possibility.

Sophocles' plot has some faults, which must be confronted frankly. To achieve his dramatic effects he has had to pay a certain price in terms of verisimilitude. We have to accept that somehow Jocasta never before discussed with Oedipus the child she and

Laius exposed, that Oedipus never mentioned the encounter at the crossroads, that neither of them ever talked about the scars on his feet, that the sole witness to Oedipus's killing of Laius was also the Herdsman to whom the infant was given for exposure, and that the Messenger from Corinth who reports Polybus's death had also received this child from the Herdsman. Critics have also been troubled by the fact that a man of Oedipus's intelligence takes so long to put two and two together to discover the truth, especially after Teiresias has told him that he was the killer, early in the play. Modern playwrights, from Corneille to Cocteau, have recast the plot to answer these questions (see Chapter 3).

We also have to accept the facts that the sole survivor and witness simply lied about how many attackers there were (118f) and that Oedipus is mistaken in thinking that he killed "all" the men escorting Laius (813).[3] And we must admit that Sophocles has left vague the amount of time that had elapsed between the killing of Laius and the witness's returning to Thebes and finding Oedipus already in place as king (758ff). During this unspecified interval (see 558ff) Oedipus has managed to defeat the Sphinx, marry Jocasta, and become installed as king of Thebes.

A play is not a novel, and *Oedipus Tyrannus*'s rhythm of action is so gripping, and the movement of human emotions so convincing, that these problems do not bother us while we watch or even read the play. If we do stop to think about them (as most viewers or readers do not), they all have plausible answers. Laius's trusted Herdsman who received the child for exposure would be a likely escort for the king on his journey to Delphi. A man who "fled in fear," as Creon says (118), at the attack on Laius would be likely to keep quiet out of fear after finding Laius's killer established as the ruler of Thebes. Being a slave, he is at Oedipus's mercy, and his timidity and vulnerability are clear when we see him interrogated by Oedipus.

Oedipus might be faulted for having neglected to investigate Laius's killing and for not even knowing where it happened (113–14). Yet the play shows that the old king's death was the Thebans' concern primarily in the period before Oedipus assumed the throne, and that they were too preoccupied with the Sphinx to carry out a full inquiry. Oedipus asks why they did not investigate more thoroughly, and he receives a satisfactory answer (128ff,

558ff). Newly installed as king of a country being ravaged by a monster, involved with a new marriage and new duties, he would naturally have been far more concerned about the future than the past. By the time of the present action, Laius's murder was regarded as past history, and this is clear from the way Oedipus speaks of the event. The Sphinx is gone; orderly succession to the throne has occurred; and Thebes has been happy, so far, with its new ruler. The old king is dead; long live the king!

Teiresias's prophetic powers also raise questions. If he has such foreknowledge, why did he not intervene to stop the marriage of Oedipus and Jocasta? Why could he not answer the riddle of the Sphinx himself, and why did he wait so many years to declare Oedipus the killer of Laius? Oedipus raises these last two questions (390–98, 558–68), and they are never answered explicitly. When Oedipus asks Creon point-blank about why Teiresias delayed so long in naming Laius's killer, Creon merely says that he does not know (569). This is probably Sophocles' way of telling us to leave the matter there; the ways of prophets are obscure, after all, and especially the ways of prophets as awesome as Teiresias.

Teiresias's foreknowledge suggests the existence of forces and patterns in our lives beyond the limit of ordinary human knowledge. As to his failure to help Thebes earlier, we have to accept it as a given piece of background detail that the Sphinx could be defeated only by the young hero from outside, not by an old prophet within. Monsters, too, have ways of their own; Sophocles, in any case, is careful to keep details about this fabulous beast very vague.[4]

Teiresias's silence, however, is a more interesting matter. Even in the play's present action, Oedipus has to force him to speak; so it is not surprising that he volunteered no information in the past, assuming that he knew the truth even then. Even if Apollo had revealed the truth to Teiresias long ago (a fact that we have no right to assume), presumably the god also revealed that he, Apollo, would bring it to light in his own sweet time.

Speculation along these lines is fruitless, and one runs the risk of the so-called documentary fallacy: treating the events as if they occur in real life and not as part of a literary construct that creates a circumscribed, artificial world. For the artifice to work, however, it has to be plausible, and the meeting between the king and the prophet is indeed plausible, both dramatically and emotionally. They interact as two such leaders might be expected to respond in a crisis involving power and authority. They are both proud, stubborn, and hot-tempered men; both are defensive, and both are led to say more than they initially intended. Oedipus, we know from the prologue, will be energetically exploring every means available to do what Apollo has commanded and find the killer. The unsolved murder of his predecessor makes him uneasy and suspicious about a conspiracy to overthrow his own regime. Teiresias, too, is not used to being contradicted, let alone accused. We may compare the irascible Teiresias of *Antigone* (1048–94) and the aged and blind Oedipus himself in *Oedipus at Colonus*.

It is part of the tragic pattern that Teiresias's very silence raises Oedipus's suspicions of his collusion with Creon, as we see when Oedipus interrogates Creon about Laius's death, the inquiry to Delphi, and Teiresias's silence in the past (555ff). Here again possible divine causation interacts naturally and plausibly with human motivation. Viewed as part of a divine plan, Teiresias's silence can be attributed to his knowledge, as a divine prophet, of what is bound to happen anyway, regardless of whether he speaks. Viewed in terms of normal human behavior (especially in the volatile political atmosphere of a late fifth-century *polis*), Oedipus is justified in assuming that Creon and Teiresias have conspired to accuse him of the murder and seize the power for themselves.

The silence of Teiresias has another and perhaps more profound meaning, and this relates not so much to character as to moral structure. His presence, like that of the oracles, implies the existence of some kind of order operating mysteriously in our world. The most general Greek term for this order is *dikê*, often translated as "justice" but actually connoting something like "path of retribution." It implies a process that undoes violence by violence. It restores a balance in the world order that has been upset by action beyond the limits of allowable human behavior, and this restoration of order may bring with it even greater suffering than the original crime. In simplest terms, the crimes of Oedipus, regardless of his moral guilt, are a source of this kind of disorder, and the violence that he has released will return to his world and his life.

The stain of blood that Oedipus carries from killing Laius, even though he acted in self-defense, is the source of a pollution that results in the plague. Sophocles' audience would naturally assume that the plague was sent by the gods, and Apollo's command, which Creon reports from Delphi in the first scene, confirms this. Sophocles, however, never actually says that the gods have sent the plague. In its mysterious and probably supernatural origin, the plague is both the causal agent of the process of purging disorder that the Greeks called *dikê* and the sign that this process is under way.

Oedipus's pollution would normally require ritual purification and exile from his city, at least for some years. The murder and incest are a source of grave pollution, but legally Oedipus is not a criminal, for he acted in self-defense in the one case and in ignorance in the second, as he argues before the citizens of Colonus in *Oedipus at Colonus* (258–74, 960–99). Unlike the later play, however, *Oedipus Tyrannus* stresses the sheer misfortune and unpredictability of Oedipus's situation, rather than questions of legality. The play clearly distinguishes between the parricide and incest that Oedipus committed in ignorance and the willed act of self-blinding when he discovers the truth (1329–46). This willed and self-chosen punishment also contrasts with his involuntary curse on himself as Laius's killer, which he pronounced early in the play (246–51). At the same time this curse becomes another of the tragic coincidences that stretch Oedipus's sufferings to their fullest possible pitch, for his own zeal to help his city dooms him even more horribly, "to wear out his wretched life wretchedly in utter doom" (248).

At a time of intense interest in issues of causality, motivation, and legality, the play explored the shadowy areas between involuntary crime, religious pollution, moral innocence, and the personal horror in feeling oneself the bearer of a terrible guilt. Oedipus is not completely innocent, but as a court of law might measure it, his suffering and the suffering of those around him (Jocasta, their children, and all those who have died in the plague) is far out of proportion to his degree of guilt. Like every great tragedy, the play forces us to rethink our comfortable assumptions about a just world order. Oedipus's tragic heroism consists in taking on himself, by his own hand, a punishment far greater than what the law would require.

The irreducible discrepancy here between what a man has done and what he suffers makes up the play's tragic view of life, a view that presents our control over our circumstances as precarious and our grasp on happiness as always uncertain. Teiresias, in his paradoxical vision-in-blindness, knows this truth but is reluctant to tell it, partly because we do not want to hear it. It is a characteristically tragic wisdom, and as such it must be wrested from him forcibly and received reluctantly, if at all.

In an old tale we find a mythical paradigm for this kind of knowledge and its difficult reception among men. Silenus, a satyr, is captured and forced to reveal his knowledge. "Why do you force me to tell what it is better for you not to know?" he asks his captors. "For life is freest of pain when it is accompanied by ignorance of its own suffering. . . . For mortals, best of all is not to be born" (Plutarch, *Consolation to Apollonius*, 115D). The reluctant silence of Teiresias is akin to the reluctance of this wise demigod of nature; Sophocles echoes the sentiments in a choral ode in his last play: "Not to be born wins every accounting; and by far second best is when born to return there whence one has come as quickly as possible" (*Oedipus at Colonus*, 1224–28).

What is at stake in Oedipus's inquiry, then, is not just his personal situation—it is also the makeup of the world and its bearing on the possibility of happiness in human life. Through Teiresias, the oracles, and the puzzlement of the chorus, questions about the orderliness, justice, or chaos of our world are framed not in the small, petty circumstances of daily life but in the large civic arena and against the background of the vast natural world. The mountains—especially Cithaeron, which reappears throughout the play, and also Parnassus and Olympus—are in the background, part of the outer frame, as are the places beyond the limits of the mortal world—especially the far western realm of death mentioned in the first ode (the parodos)—and the eternal realm of the gods and their laws, spoken of in the third ode (the second stasimon).

STORY AND PLOT

In looking at the remarkable design of *Oedipus Tyrannus* we must distinguish not only between the play and the myth but also between the *story* (the totality of the events as they might be told in chronological order) and the *plot* (the events as they appear in the order shown in the play). This play does not tell the whole myth of Oedipus, nor even the whole story of his life; it unfolds as a *plot*, a carefully chosen and constructed sequence of events at one brief, though decisive, crisis in the hero's life. From that point the play moves both backward and forward to other parts of the myth as a whole. The plot does not give us all the details at once, nor does it present them in a continuous order or as a single, linear development. It reveals fragments, and we, like Oedipus, have to piece these together to make up a coherent narrative.

It is characteristic of Sophocles' selective narration that he reserves his most focused, continuous account of events for the few tense moments surrounding Jocasta's death and Oedipus's self-blinding (1237–85). There is no connected story of Oedipus's life, from his birth to his rule at Thebes, such as Euripides provides in the prologue of his *Phoenician Women*. Instead, the past of Oedipus is a shadowy area of elusive facts submerged in what seems to be remote, mythic time.

The plot structure has two other related effects. First, the events of the past are surrounded by mystery both because they are so remote and so horrible and because they are recovered so gradually and so painfully. Second, the *process* of the discovery is as important as the *content* of what is discovered. This is a play about how we uncover a hidden, horrible, and frightening past. The rhythm of this process of discovery gives the play its unique power and fascination.

The play's most powerful moments come when the search for knowledge takes two different directions simultaneously. This happens first near the exact center of the play. Jocasta, intending to turn Oedipus away from further pursuit of Teiresias's prophecy, gives him the clue about the triple road that in fact intensifies his search. Later the pattern is repeated when the Messenger inadvertently deflects Oedipus from the search for Laius's killer to the search for his own parents. At the end of this scene, Jocasta urges him not to carry his investigation any further (1056ff), whereas Oedipus is determined to press on, ignorant that the answer to both searches is the same. The following scene closes that gap between the two searches; but to reach that moment of "terrible hearing" (1169) Oedipus has to wrest knowledge forcibly from one who refuses to tell. It is part of the play's irony that the same action that led to triumph in the past—namely, overcoming the resistance of one who knows but will not tell (the Sphinx)—now leads to total disaster.

TELLING THE STORY BACKWARD: REVERSIBLE TIME

Oedipus Tyrannus is almost unique among Greek tragedies in telling its story in reverse. Nearly every crucial event in the action has already happened. The action is therefore almost all retrospective action—that is, it depicts how the characters (and the spectators too) see and understand in the present events that took place far in the past. For this purpose, too, the play uses and scrutinizes the different ways in which stories unfold, the different ways in which one may tell one's life story, and the different ways in which such stories are heard and understood. The chief events of Oedipus's life history—his birth, exposure, victories over Laius and the Sphinx, and marriage—emerge piecemeal, from different points of view and in partial, fragmented perspective. Like Oedipus, we as spectators have to reconstruct a hidden past from hints, memories, glimpses.

Because of this way of telling its story, the play is also about narrative. It uses the special ability of literary texts to reflect on their own artifice and to remind us of the ways in which they can suspend reality to offer an enhanced vision of reality. One of Sophocles' contemporaries, the philosopher and rhetorician Gorgias, wrote, apropos of the effect of tragedy, "He who deceives is more just than he who does not deceive, and the one deceived is wiser than the one who is not deceived."[5] In the case of *Oedipus Tyrannus*, the "wisdom" that we (the "deceived" audience) get comes from accepting the dramatic illusion (the "deception" of the plot) and participating in the special vision of the world that we thus receive. At the same time we know that this vision is real only in a particular sense, as a model of a problem or a hypothesis about our world that we rarely see so sharply focused in our everyday reality.

As part of its wise deception the play also exploits its freedom to tell its story in fragments, in scenes taken out of chronological order, with omissions that are filled in later, and in flashbacks. Art has the power to reverse time and to let us see and question modes of causality that are invisible in real life. We are forced to think about the role of the gods and, especially, the mixture of free choice and necessity in the oracles. If Laius, Jocasta, and Oedipus, for example, had done nothing to avoid the oracles, would they have come true anyway? Or by taking their evasive action did they, in fact, play into the hands of the gods and bring about the very events that they were trying to prevent? The literary device of telling events out of their chronological order also creates much of Sophocles' celebrated irony: the discrepancy between the larger picture that we, the spectators, see and the small piece visible to the actor who is immersed in the stream of events.

It is revealing to compare Oedipus's story with that of Odysseus, another hero whose myth embraces the whole of a life cycle. The dominant feature of Odysseus's story, as we see it in Homer's *Odyssey*, is commitment to the return, a successful and ultimately happy journey home, with a clear goal and strong emphasis on the motifs of regaining and rebirth. The dominant feature of Oedipus's story is the tragic shape of a life that is always turning back on itself instead of going forward.

The continuity in the *Odyssey* corresponds to the clarity and forward movement of narrative in the epic form, in contrast to the halting, unpredictable, blocked movements of narrative in tragedy.[6] In the expansive epic frame, narrative is relatively unproblematic because time is unproblematic. Although the *Odyssey* uses retrospective narration (in the flashback of books 9–12), the hero's movement in time is steadily forward, toward his goal. Even when Odysseus regains his former life, past and present are clearly distinguished. In tragedy, and especially in *Oedipus Tyrannus*, time is constantly bending backward and forward with mysterious gaps and discontinuities. The dangers and limits that surround human life in tragedy make both generational time and narrative time uncertain, unreliable, and complicated. Even though the recognition of the limits of mortality is a major theme in the tale of Odysseus, he is always able to see, and ultimately to achieve, his goal of returning to the full life he left behind. For Oedipus, past and future are always getting entangled with each other. In the terrible circularity of his life pattern, he can never pull free of the maimed life in the past.

The almost simultaneous return of the Messenger and the Herdsman, who together saved the baby Oedipus many years ago, seems like pure coincidence, but on reflection this reveals a "coincidence" of another kind. Such returns are appropriate to a life story that cannot break free of its past. The past is always returning, in the wrong place. The child returns to the bed and to the "furrows" of his mother, "sowing" where he was "plowed," as Oedipus cries out in his agony near the end (1403ff). The son cast out by the father comes back to meet the father in just the wrong place and so to kill him. The oracle originally given to Laius keeps returning, different yet always the same, to mark the different stages of Oedipus's life: in infancy, at the end of his adolescence, and in his maturity, when he is king of Thebes. Even a slave at the periphery of a famed king's life turns out to be a part of a mysterious rhythm of fatally overlapping returns. The Herdsman who saved the infant Oedipus reappears at his passage between adolescence and adulthood to witness his killing of Laius, and then again at his tragic passage from full maturity to the blindness and debility of his remaining years. Sophocles does not use these coincidences as proof of a deterministic universe, but rather as the facts of an uncanny pattern of a life that is thus marked as tragic.

TIME, ORACLE, AND RIDDLE

The riddle has the opposite role from the oracle in Oedipus's life: it is a source of pride and confidence, whereas the oracle is a source of anxiety and helplessness. He can resolve the simultaneity of the various stages of life intellectually, in the *verbal* play of the riddle, but he acts out the horror of that fusion of separate generational stages in living a *life* that fulfills the oracle.

While the answer to the riddle implies the complete span of a full life, from infancy to old age, the oracle would prevent this life from getting started at all. In the form in which it is given to Laius, it would first prevent a child's begetting and then prevent his growing up. Oedipus solved the riddle by seeing through its metaphor of feet for motion through life. But of course his own feet hold the secret or riddle of his life, and that is partly because of the oracle, which led his parents to bind his feet together into one so that he, unlike the creeping, walking, and cane-using generic man of the riddle, would never walk at all, never move through any of the stages of life.

The circular movement of time in the play itself is governed by the oracles. The first oracle is in the present: the command from Apollo at Delphi to drive out the land's pollution, the cause of the plague. It is an order and thus is directed to the future, but of course it points us back to the past, to the killing of Laius nearly 20 years ago. The second oracle, given to Laius and Jocasta, referred to future events: the father will die at the hands of his son. But at the point when Jocasta tells Oedipus about this oracle, it belongs to the remote past (711–23). And Oedipus fears his own oracle, the play's third, which he received at Delphi many years before, as pointing to his future. But when he relates it to Jocasta (787–93) it is in fact already part of his past: he has already fulfilled it in his journey from Delphi to Thebes.

Measuring and counting time is one of Oedipus's major actions onstage. His attempts to organize time into logical patterns, however, collapse in the terrible uncertainty of time in his own life. Rather than serving as something he can find out and know with certainty, time becomes an active force that finally has "found him out" as the one who long ago joined that "no-marriage marriage" in which "birth and begetting," origins and maturity, were fused together (1213–15). Rather than being an aid to human understanding, time seems to have a kind of independent power that blocks knowledge. It blocks future knowledge because its course has been hidden from the actors. It blocks past knowledge because memory selects and filters. Both the Messenger of the blinding scene and the Herdsman attribute this failure of knowledge to erroneous or partial memory. Even Oedipus cannot accurately remember the details of his fatal encounter with Laius. As we now know, he did not kill all of the travelers.

Time in the play expands and contracts, producing effects of vagueness or density by turns. It is both the indefinite and inert passing of years and the single moment of crisis in decision and action, the irreversible turning point of a man's life. When he can still hope that the truth will leave his present view of himself intact, Oedipus describes himself as defined by his "kindred months" in a slow rhythm of waxing and waning, becoming small and great (1082f). But in fact he is defined by the abrupt catastrophe of a single day (351, 438), which makes him both great and small, king and beggar, in one instant.

Time can have an unexpected fullness, as in Creon's account of past events in the prologue. Here there seems to be an indefinite interval between the death of Laius and the arrival of Oedipus to vanquish the Sphinx, an interval in which the Thebans cannot investigate the death of their king because the Sphinx compels them to consider only the immediate present, "to regard the things at our feet, letting go the things unclear" (130–31). It is as if this major crisis in the present life of the city retreats to the obscurity of remote happenings, far beyond living memory. But Oedipus, in his confident belief that he can overcome time, announces, "But *I* shall bring these things to light *from their beginning*" (132; my italics).

When Oedipus thinks that he has in fact reached through time to reveal the hidden truth, the time surrounding Laius's death again has the same vagueness and fullness. Interrogating Creon, whom he now takes to be the agent of the murder, Oedipus asks, "How much time before did Laius [die]?" and Creon replies, "Times [or, years] great and old would be measured" (561). As in the prologue, that critical event, the death of the king and the father, becomes surrounded by an aura of remote, almost mythical time, as if it were an act belonging to primordial beginnings (as in one sense it did) and not to a specific historical moment in the life of an individual and a city.

Oedipus is confident that he will uncover these beginnings, but origins are more mysterious and harder to fathom than he knows. At the climactic moment of discovery this vague temporal duration is suddenly ripped open by the electrifying flash of the single moment of "terrible hearing" (1169). In the relaxed seasonal tempo of the Herdsman's life on Cithaeron, before Oedipus's birth, only the changes of summer and winter, without events, mark the passage of time (1132ff). But tragic time has a wholly different aspect: it is the single instant of decision and recognition that suddenly overturns an entire life.

88

It is a gift of prophetic knowledge to see time past, present, and future in a single vision. Calchas in the *Iliad* "knew what is and what will be and what is before" (*Iliad*, 1.70); the prophet Theonoe in Euripides' *Helen* "understood the divine things, those now and all those to come" (*Helen*, 13–14). In *Oedipus Tyrannus* the audience first sees Oedipus in the present as king and ruler, supplicated by his people because they hope he will save them. But Teiresias, a little later, sees the Oedipus of the future, a blind man tapping his way with his stick. Jocasta and the Herdsman see Oedipus as a helpless newborn, his feet pierced so that no one will take him up. Jocasta, again, in her last words on stage, sees the whole course of Oedipus's life as one of utter misery, which she marks in her final words for him, "ill-fated" and "unfortunate" (1068, 1071). The spectator at the play enjoys the omniscient perspective of the gods; like the gods, he or she can see Oedipus in all three roles at once: the powerful king, the accursed and helpless infant, and the blinded sufferer.

TRACKING THE PAST: THE RETURN OF THE REPRESSED

Knowledge, in the play, results from bringing separate, individual past events together into a single moment in the present. The major action of the play gets under way with Oedipus's inquiry about Laius's murder: "Where will be found this trace, hard to track, of the ancient crime?" (108–9). The investigation is like a hunt, and Oedipus assumes that he can follow a set of tracks that will lead smoothly from the present to the past, Laius's past. But the road into the past proves not to be single but manifold, just as Oedipus himself proves to be not one but many. Thus, instead of the track leading to only one object of inquiry, Laius's killer, it in fact diverges into several different paths—triple roads, one could say: Oedipus's origins, his exposure by his parents, his marriage to Jocasta.

This collocation of the past with the present receives vivid dramatic enactment in nearly every scene of the play. Indeed, the very first line of the play, Oedipus's address to the suppliant citizens, juxtaposes old and new: "O children, of Cadmus old the newest brood." Visually, too, this scene displays a combination of ages, in the onstage presence of youths, mature men, and elders, as the priest explains a few lines later (15–19). Oedipus is himself an anomalous composite of young and old, since the incest makes him the member of two generations simultaneously.

This combination of past and present again becomes ominously vivid in Teiresias, the old man who belongs to the past and sees the truth that threads the past together with the future. "The future events will come of themselves," he says at the beginning of his interview with Oedipus, "even if I conceal them in silence" (341). Instead of thus concealing the future he brings it visually before our eyes in his dreadful prophecies. Although he is not understood by Oedipus in the present, Teiresias warns him that he does not see "where he is" (367, 413ff) or the future sufferings that await him (427–29, 453ff). Those sufferings consist precisely in the fact that the incest makes the father "equal" to his children (424) and removes the boundaries that should separate those stages and activities of life (456–60).

Oedipus's intelligence, Jocasta suggests later, lies in "inferring the new by means of the old" (916). When Oedipus does in fact bring together the old things of his remote infancy and early manhood with the new things of his present life and circumstances, he knows himself as both king and pollution, both the savior and the destroyer of Thebes.

As Oedipus begins his tracking of Laius's killer (109) he needs, as he says, a *symbolon* (221), a word usually translated "clue." But the word also means a "tally," one of two parts of a token that fit together to prove one's rightful place. In Sophocles' day, Athenians used such tokens for admission to the law courts. The investigative skill that Oedipus will demonstrate, then, consists in fitting pieces together. The word *symbolon* also has another meaning, as the "token" left with a child exposed at birth, to establish later proof of his identity. The word carries this sense in the tale of Ion, another foundling, dramatized in Euripides' *Ion*—a kind of Oedipus story in reverse. Presented with an old basket that contains the secret of his origins, Ion hesitates to open it and examine the "tokens from his mother" (*Ion*, 1386) lest he turn out to be the child of a slave (1382–83: see also *Oedipus Tyrannus*, 1063, 1168). He finally decides to take the risk ("I must dare" [*Ion*, 1387]), just as Oedipus does ("I must hear" [1170]), although with very different results. Oedipus's initially objective, public task of tracking down a killer by a clue (*symbolon* in the juridical sense) turns into the personal and intimate task of finding the birth-token (*symbolon* in the personal sense) that proves his identity.

As the forward rhythm of the push for knowledge begins to accelerate, there is a retarding movement that pulls back toward not knowing, toward leaving origins veiled in darkness. It is appropriately the mother who takes on this retarding role. She who stood at the beginning of his life and (as we learn) was involved in a contradictory pull between the birth and the death of her new child (1173–75), would still keep him from the terrible knowledge and thus save his life. Like all great plots, the play combines forward movement to the end with the pleasure of delaying and complicating that end.[7]

This simultaneity of past and present belongs to the uncanny or the inexplicable, which is represented onstage in the blind prophet, behind whom stands the remote and mysterious Apollo. Although Oedipus's first act is to consult Apollo at Delphi, he never integrates what Apollo and Teiresias know into what he knows. Not until it is too late does he put the oracles together by means of that intelligence whose special property is to join past and present, to connect disparate events, facts, experiences, stages of life. His failure in logical deduction was one of Voltaire's objections to the structure of the play.[8] But what an Enlightenment rationalist would consider a fault an ancient dramatist would consider the very essence of the tragic element. Oedipus uses his human knowledge primarily in conflict with the divine, to block, deny, contradict, or evade it.

Knowledge veers not only between human and divine, but also between active and passive. Human knowledge is actively sought as the achievement of man's intellectual power; divine knowledge comes, it seems, by chance, on precarious and unpredictable paths. The divine knowledge of Teiresias's prophecy is confirmed only by sheer coincidence, in the form of the Messenger and the Herdsman, and it is the latter who provides the clinching piece of knowledge, Oedipus's identity as the exposed child of Laius and Jocasta.

The first mention of the one person who "knows" anything is as vague as possible: the man is only "some one man" (118). Oedipus makes no attempt to refine this description. Instead he shifts attention from "some one *man*" to "some one *thing*" in his next line: "What sort of thing [did he say]? For one thing would find out many things for learning" (120). The grammatical categories of language itself—the ease of shifting from masculine to neuter (one man, one thing) and from singular to plural (robber, robbers)—lead the investigators astray from what will finally solve the mystery. Language itself encourages their deception and causes them to pursue what will prove to be, in one sense, misinformation.

Forgotten for some 600 lines, more than a third of the play, this individual resurfaces when Jocasta's reference to the triple roads (another numerical problem) arouses Oedipus's anxiety (see 730). "Alas, these things are now clear," he says. "Who was it who spoke these words to you, my wife?" (754–55). "A house-servant," Jocasta replies, "who arrived as the only one saved" (756). This last phrase is the other, objective side of Creon's more subjectively oriented description of the man as "having fled in fear" in the prologue (118).

"Did he then happen to be present in the house?" Oedipus presses on. "No," answers Jocasta, and she explains how the servant came to Thebes, found Oedipus already in possession of the royal power and Laius dead. Touching Jocasta's hand, he asked to be sent to the fields (761) and to the pastures of the flocks, so that "he might be as far as possible out of sight of the town" (755–82). The contrast between "house" and "field" (756–61) recalls Oedipus's first specific point of investigation in Laius's death: "Was it in the house or in the fields?" (112). The sole witness there was "some one man" (118); and Creon's phrase calls attention to his unitary identity. His initial "oneness," like that of Oedipus, bifurcates ominously into two. He is both the house servant (756) and the herdsman in the "pastures of the flocks" (761). He is both the man described by Jocasta and the man described by Creon, both the man who survived the attack on Laius and the killer/rescuer of the infant Oedipus on Cithaeron. Like Oedipus, he is both an insider ("reared in the house," as he describes himself later [1123]) and an outsider, one who was sent from the house to the fields or the mountains.

This figure of the Herdsman/Escort plays an increasingly important role in giving different perspectives on what really happened in the past. He possesses "knowing" (*eidôs*) from a crucial "seeing" (*eide*, 119), a play on the similarity between the Greek words that is not easily translated into English. But here, as throughout the drama, this wordplay is charged with meaning. At this early point in the work, when Creon mentions the lone survivor for the first time, his reported story introduces the identification of knowing with seeing that is central to the play's concern with ignorance and perception. Later Jocasta tells Oedipus that it was after the Herdsman "saw" Oedipus on the throne that he requested from her a kind of absence of vision, to be "out of sight of the house" (762). Like Oedipus in the future, he seeks a combination of negated vision ("out of the sight of the house") and exile from his place in house and city (see 1384–94, 1451–54).

Still confident as the king searching for the killer of Laius, Oedipus then sends for this only survivor of the attack on the former king (765–770). It is sheer coincidence that this man should also be the one whom Laius entrusted with killing the infant Oedipus. And yet that coincidence points to a deep necessity. Oedipus cannot progress in his role as ruler of the city, whose task it is to discover and expel Laius's killer, until he has solved the mystery of his own origins. He cannot solve the mystery of the plague until he solves the mystery of himself. To do that, he has to force the figure who holds the missing piece to recapitulate earlier stages of his life as well: when he changed from house servant (756) to herdsman (761), and when, in the earlier role, he had brought Oedipus to both doom and salvation on Mount Cithaeron (see 1349–52). The philosopher George Santayana remarked that those who do not know history are compelled to repeat it. *Oedipus Tyrannus* works out the truth of this statement on the level of personal history: not to know who you are is to be compelled to search ceaselessly for your origins.

The Herdsman's life also parallels Oedipus's in the spatial shift that he undergoes in the course of the play, from house to mountain, from a figure at the center of the palace life (756) to a figure at the margins of the city, in the mountains. The Herdsman's life, governed by such different rhythms of space and time, proves to be causally related to Oedipus's life and also similar to it in form, parallel in its course but also more vaguely outlined and set into a larger and remoter frame. The condensation of Oedipus's life into the hour or two acted out in the time of the performance has behind it, like a larger shadow, the more expansive movement of the Herdsman's passage through time.

The Herdsman recurs as a figure dimly parallel to Oedipus in his life's movements and spontaneous impulses of pity and fear. The first specific detail given about him is his "flight in fear," to be "the only one saved" (118, 756). His characteristic mode of action in the play is evasion through running away. This is what he did when Oedipus attacked Laius at the crossroads and what he did again when he returned from that episode to find Oedipus ruling in Thebes. It is also what the young Oedipus did when he heard his destiny foretold him at Delphi (788–97). The Herdsman repeats the pattern a third and last time on the stage when Oedipus interrogates him. He tries to escape by evasion or denial (see 1129–31, 1146–59, 1165), but now Oedipus compels him to face and speak the "terrible" that is contained in the truth (1169–70).

This last scene brings Oedipus and his shadowy double together, finally, on the stage. Now neither of them can run away. Yet this coming together shows us their characteristic divergence. The Herdsman is a slave (see 1123; also 764, 1168), and he seeks survival by denying the truth. The king goes to meet his destiny head-on, confronting the necessity that comes from the oracles surrounding his existence, even if that confrontation means his death. The Herdsman at the crossroads was "the only one to be saved" (756). King Oedipus is ready to become the sacrificial victim, the *pharmakos* or scapegoat, whose single death saves the whole city (see 1409ff).[9]

A READING

✤

8

The Crisis of the City
and the King

PROLOGUE AND PARODE

The opening scene or prologue (i.e., everything before the entrance of the chorus at line 151) is brilliantly constructed. Quickly and economically Sophocles leads us into the city's crisis, provides the essential details to orient us in the present, and lets us see the chief protagonist in action. Nothing seems superfluous. The background emerges from the situation itself. But behind the clarity of exposition lie many unknowns: the remote death of Laius, the Sphinx, Apollo, and of course the awful truth that is hinted at in the ironies and the double meanings, as when Oedipus pledges that he will be "removing the pollution not in behalf of remoter kin but for my very self" (137–38).

The play opens with Oedipus standing before a group of citizens who carry the insignia of ritual supplication. They have come to him, their ruler and protector, for help against the ravages of the plague. The visual configuration establishes him in his role as king, the protector of his people.[1] His brief speech of comfort, the first words of the play (1–13), establishes quickly and specifically some basic traits of his character: his concern for the city and its inhabitants, his reverence for the marks of supplication, his compassion for the young and helpless, his energy and good will. These impressions are confirmed by the Priest, the spokesman for the suppliants, who addresses the king with hope and confidence in his power, recalling his previous successes, particularly in defeating the Sphinx. They regard him as their savior, almost as a god (48), and Oedipus responds to the challenge with compassion, commitment, and energy.

This is the only surviving play of Sophocles that begins with such a mass scene—an effect more common in Aeschylus and Euripides. Generally Sophocles begins with a quieter, more private setting, a monologue or a close conversation between two characters (as in *Antigone* and *Oedipus at Colonus*). The public nature of the opening of *Oedipus Tyrannus* calls attention both to the danger facing the entire city and to Oedipus's responsibility as the leader who confronts that danger and takes it upon himself.

The opening scene has still another function. The rite of supplication implies the acknowledgment of another's greater power, in this case that of the gods, but the recognition of helplessness before the gods is combined with the city's confidence in the power of a mortal, Oedipus. The Priest, a man of traditional piety, is concerned to distinguish his supplication of Oedipus from that of a god and thus introduces one of the central issues, mortal limitation and divine power:

> We have not come as suppliants to this altar
> because we thought of you as of a God,
> but rather judging you the first of men
> in all the chances of this life and when
> we mortals have to do with more than man.
> (Grene's translation, 31–34)

There is a warning note in the phrase "first of men in all the chances of this life" (33), for this can also mean, "first of men in the misfortunes of life." In fact the word translated as "chances" (*symphorai*) refers to the extreme "misfortunes" of Oedipus where it recurs in three later passages (833, 1347, 1527). The phrase thus foreshadows the extremes of success and misery that Oedipus will span as the exemplar of mortal vicissitude.

Supplication is usually addressed to a god; this is one of the rare places in extant Greek tragedy where the protagonist is the one to be supplicated rather than the one to supplicate (as in Euripides' *Hecuba*) or merely to receive the suppliants (as in Aeschylus's *Sup-*

pliants). This situation not only exalts Oedipus but also helps prepare for the major reversal in the plot, the shift from the collective
crisis of Thebes to the personal crisis of its ruler.

At the same time the Priest's collocation of old and young, boys
and mature men (16ff) sets forth that coincidence of different stages
of life that will come to define Oedipus in his unique disaster. When
he answers the Priest's appeal, he restates the combination of one
and many, knowledge and ignorance, wholeness and infirmity that
will eventually define the tragic shape of his life:

> . . . *I know* you are *all* sick
> yet there is *not one* of you, *sick* though you are,
> that is as *sick as I myself.*
> Your *several* sorrows each have *single* scope
> and touch *but one* of you. *My* spirit groans
> for *city and myself and you at once.*
>> (Grene's translation, 59–64; my italics)

Oedipus's identification of his own suffering with the city's conceals
his status as the polluted criminal who can heal the city's disease.
When he goes on to speak of the "many roads of thought" that he
has traveled to arrive at the "only cure" for the plague (67–69), we
are prepared for the literal roads that he has traversed in reaching
Thebes, especially the road where he met and killed Laius (801–4),
thus bringing into the city its present "disease," which is himself.

Although Sophocles begins the play with the focus on Oedipus,
he also makes us aware of the world around Oedipus, above all the
city and the spaces of the city, both sacred and secular, both within
and outside the walls. The Priest evokes the civic population gath-
ered in the marketplace. He mentions the two temples of Athena
and the oracular shrine of Apollo by the river Ismenus (20–21). He
speaks of the fields and the fertile earth and the cattle in the pastures, all blighted by the plague. The words *city* and *town* recur
repeatedly. But all of this human space is intersected by another
realm, that of the gods above, who have sent the plague, and the
gods below, to whom the Priest refers when he tells how "black
Hades grows rich with the groans and cries of lament" (25–30).
Images of the sea, which recur throughout the play, also suggest
the great powers of nature mastered by human intelligence but
always uncertain and dangerous (see 23–24, 50–51).

The Priest takes us beyond the present in his allusions to Oedipus's earlier liberation of the city from its troubles in defeating the Sphinx (35–36), the deed that gave him that universal "fame" which he proudly mentions in his opening speech (7–8): "I have come myself, I who am called Oedipus famous to all." Oedipus's announcement that he has already sent Creon to Delphi to seek a remedy from Apollo's oracle gives solid proof of his energy and concern (68–72), but throughout the speech (58–79) he also uses those images of walking, disease, time, knowledge, and revealing that will resonate ominously through the rest of the play.

Reckoning the time of Creon's absence, Oedipus gives a hint of his impatient energy. As Creon enters (for the play has no time to waste), Oedipus speaks of his eye and his walking, while the Priest points out the garlands of laurel, a sign of good fortune (78–84). Both men hang on Creon's words, but the priest now steps aside and Oedipus takes the commanding role, conducting the first of the several interrogations that make up the action of the play.

The little dialogue between Oedipus and Creon is a miniature instance of that "encounter with the divine" in which the Priest had just praised Oedipus, and the king lives up to his best hopes. He literally does not lose a moment. He is attentive and neither too confident nor too fearful (89–90)—which provides a point of reference for his swings between these opposite moods later in the play (913–17). Concerned about all his people, he insists that the oracle be announced publicly, to all, not kept as a state secret among the leaders (91–94). When he hears that Apollo's command is "to drive out the land's pollution and not nurture it unhealed," he at once searches for the remedy in clipped and eager questions (99): "By what purification? What is the character of the misfortune?" Yet the metaphor of "nurture" that Creon reports as Apollo's word ("the pollution nurtured in this land") points to that realm of birth and family that is so fraught with pain and peril for Oedipus.

The polluted killer, Creon reports, must be driven into exile or punished by death. The choice between exile or death will return later in the play, particularly when Oedipus accuses Creon of the crime and opts for the harsher penalty (622–23). Since Oedipus will not be put to death at the end of the play, it is also necessary to have the lighter punishment in view. Oedipus himself envisages only exile when he refers to this punishment later (823–24, 1379–82).

In reporting Apollo's reply, Creon also uses the language of retributive justice, expiating "killing by killing in return, since a storm of blood rages upon the city" (100–1). The solemnity of the repetition, "killing by killing," is appropriate to the god and evokes archaic notions of retribution: blood must be paid for by blood. The metaphor of the "storm of blood upon the city" also points to the interconnectedness of the human community ("city") with the mysterious forces of nature ("storm"), here evident in the plague. At the same time, it foreshadows the "black rain and bloody hail"—also metaphorical—that fall from Oedipus's eyes when he blinds himself in punishment for the pollution (1278–80), thus fulfilling the god's command of "blood for blood."

With the rapid exchange of Oedipus's questions and Creon's short replies, the play moves into its major mode of action, the recovery of a buried past (102–31). Oedipus swiftly elicits the scant but important details of Laius's death, and we see at once how he would have pursued such an investigation in the past. As the dim and fragmentary facts emerge, the errors and omissions are intermingled with truth. Laius was killed on a sacred journey (114–15), Creon reports, but he mentions neither Delphi nor the crossroads.[2] These crucial details are reserved for later. Particularly striking is the vacillation between singular and plural in the account of the event (97, 108, 118–24). Although Creon lays heavy stress on the plural, "robbers," referring to Laius's killers, Oedipus asks about a single "robber." The phrase can be read as Sophoclean irony or as a Freudian slip, the surfacing of something that Oedipus knows but has suppressed.

If Oedipus's insistence on the single robber belongs to the nonrational side of mental functioning, his rational side is nevertheless fully in evidence. He makes a rapid calculation of possible intrigue within the city (125–26), which he realizes can be repeated against himself (139–41). These deductions are plausible and appropriate to a Greek city of Sophocles' time, and they explain the king's suspicions of Creon and Teiresias later. But Oedipus is not only an astute politician; he is also a decent, pious, and responsible ruler. He graciously thanks Creon, restates his determination to help, and recognizes the need for the gods' aid in his exit line (145–46): "For with the god we shall be shown as fortunate or as fallen low." The choice of words points ahead with tragic irony to his own fall, which of course takes place "with the god." "We shall be shown" also continues the imagery of revelation that so dominates the tragic reversal. "I shall show these things from the beginning," he had said confidently a few lines before, using the same word (132).

The strong echo of the opening in Oedipus's address to the Priest creates a formal closure (142ff). The Priest, satisfied with Oedipus's response, leads the suppliants away and ends with a prayer to Apollo: "May Phoebus Apollo who sent these oracles, come as both savior and healer of the disease" (149–50). Thus both Oedipus and the Priest end with references to the god, but with a characteristic difference. Oedipus speaks in the first person of his own success or failure; the Priest utters a prayer for deliverance. How one fares in such "encounters with the gods," where the priest had earlier judged Oedipus as "first of men" (34), frames the scene. By beginning and ending with the suppliants, the scene has shown the city poised between the human and the divine, protected by its temples but also at the limits of its ability to deal with the unknown forces of the gods and nature that threaten it.

The dangers and uncertainties of the realm beyond human control dominate the first ode—the parode or parodos—sung by the chorus of Theban elders. The ode's lyrical form and language give emotional expression to the fears and anxieties revealed in the opening ritual of supplication. The chorus sings of the plague on crops, cattle, and human births and makes formal prayers to the gods. We see the entire community threatened by extinction as its environment refuses to support life.

The ode has the structure and function of an apotropaic prayer—a prayer to turn away evil from the city. It thus reinforces the ritual quality of the first scene, heightens the seriousness of the city's crisis, and conveys the reality of powerful and dangerous divine forces interfering with human life. Ironically, what has to be driven away from the city is not the "raging" Thracian Ares (190–97) but the most respected man within Thebes.

In contrast to Oedipus's confidence, the elders feel defenseless: they have no "sword of thought" to fight off the disease (170–71). Their hope is almost wholly in the gods, as they take us from one sacred place to another, from their opening mention of Apollo's oracle at Delphi to the temples of Thebes (149–61). But they also evoke the demonic, hostile realms beyond the city: the western zone, beyond the sea, associated with Hades and death (175–79); the remote northern seas of Ares, where they hope that the force of the plague may be deflected (190–99). They end with prayers to their local god, Dionysus, whose torchlight processions contrast with the destructive fires of Ares and the plague (213–15; see 27, 167, 175–77, 192).

FIRST EPISODE

Oedipus responds to their prayers with a series of powerful curses on the killer and on anyone who shelters him. The curses afford ample scope for tragic irony. As in the prologue, he speaks of a single "killer," but he adds the qualification, "whether it is one or many" (246–47). He will speak of a single perpetrator again in line 293.[3] Oedipus extends his imprecation to include a possible killer "from another land" (230) who is, of course, himself. Indeed, this same phrase, "another land," will recur, in exactly the same verse position, when he learns how he owes his life to being sent away "to another land" (1178). It is a still deeper irony that the "pollution nurtured in this land," according to the oracle from Delphi (96–97), rests with the very man who was sent away, without an infant's nurture, "to another land" to avoid just such a pollution.

Just after pronouncing the curses, Oedipus criticizes the Thebans: "For even if the matter had not been urged on by a god, it was not fitting for you to leave it so uncleansed" (255–56). But Oedipus has lived uncleansed of his pollutions for all these years of his rule and marriage at Thebes. Following this reference to the uncleansed pollution, in fact, he alludes, unwittingly, to the sources of that pollution: he would have "children of the same sowing" with Laius had he lived, and he fights for the dead Laius "as for my father" (260–65). The irony is heavy, perhaps too heavy for our taste, and rather gruesome, but the figurative language keeps the horror at an appropriate distance. The ironies also help prepare us for the scene with Teiresias, who will speak openly of these hidden relationships.

In this irony-charged language of "seeds" and sharing, Oedipus makes his first reference to Jocasta:

> . . . I possess his bed
> and a wife who shares our seed . . . why, our seed
> might be the same, children born of the same mother
> might have created blood-bonds between us
> if his hope of offspring had not met disaster.
> (Fagles's translation, 260–62)

The phrase "wife who shares our seed" is another relentless play on the incest. It not only holds the truth that he and Laius have had children by the same woman, but it can also mean "woman [or wife] who has her sowing in common with her child." Teiresias will use a similar expression, again with deliberate and horrible ambiguity, to mean "the one who sows the same woman as his father did" (459–60).

The slowly built-up ironies of the hidden truth explode in Oedipus's encounter with Teiresias (297–462). Strictly speaking, the scene is not necessary for the plot, but it serves to create suspense, to show us a less self-controlled Oedipus, to awaken the anxieties that come to dominate the mood of the second half of the play, and to suggest the workings of supernatural powers. Just before Teiresias's entrance, Oedipus acknowledges the limitations of mortals before the gods, for "no man would be able to compel the gods to do what they do not wish" (280–81). The other side of that observation also holds true—namely, that the gods reveal things in their own good time, as Oedipus will learn.

As the chorus sees the blind prophet approaching, it describes him as "the only man in whom truth is inborn by nature" (299). "Truth" dominates the scene, in its contrast both with the illusion that Teiresias reveals surrounding Oedipus and with the falsehood of which Oedipus will accuse him (386ff). But if Teiresias is only a man with an inborn vision of truth, Oedipus nevertheless addresses him with extreme respect, almost as a god (300–315). The chorus refers to Teiresias as "the divine prophet" (298), and Oedipus likewise calls him "lord" and "savior." Indeed, he reminds us of the city's supplication to himself in the opening scene, for he approaches Teiresias virtually as a suppliant, with a triple repetition of the verb "save" (311–12).

As the concerned and pious ruler, Oedipus has placed great hopes in the famed prophet. When instead of offering help Teiresias asks to be sent home again, Oedipus is naturally puzzled and reiterates the city's need and supplication (322–27). "Do you plan, then, to betray us and destroy the city?" he asks finally. Only after Teiresias's point-blank refusal does Oedipus get exasperated. The change from respect to insult is very fast: "O you basest of the base," he cries to the prophet, "for you would anger even a stone, will you not speak? Will you show yourself thus unmovable and impossible?" (334–36). With effort Oedipus keeps his rising temper under control, until Teiresias again confronts him with a flat refusal (344–45). Oedipus has held back anger; Teiresias has held back truth (350, 356). Now they both let go, and Teiresias speaks out his truth—namely, that Oedipus is the source of the pollution.

The scene is often read as evidence for a tragic flaw of anger in Oedipus, or as a hint of the tyrannical behavior that the chorus warns against in general terms later, in the second stasimon (873–97), but this view is not tenable. To be sure, Oedipus is impetuous, quick-tempered, and emotional, but he behaves initially with restraint, and his anger, though unfortunate given the results, is pardonable. With the city in such danger, the prophet's refusal to speak looks incriminating, and Oedipus has already wondered earlier about a conspiracy (124–25, 139–41). He has also mentioned that the plan to call Teiresias originated with Creon (288), on whom Oedipus will now turn his suspicious eye. Teiresias, moreover, has been just as irascible as Oedipus. (Indeed, angry old men are a common feature of Sophoclean drama: compare the Teiresias of *Antigone* and the aged Oedipus of *Oedipus at Colonus*.)

Temperament and circumstances work together with the prophet's supernatural knowledge to shape the event. A calmer, more submissive, or more timid man—Creon, for example—might have taken Teiresias's refusal at face value and just let him go home. Oedipus is not the man to give up so easily. The irony of the situation is that with all their shouting these two gifted men speak past each other. When the truth is spoken, it cannot be heard. Oedipus is not yet ready to receive the truth, and the anger in Teiresias's telling sets up so much interference that Oedipus cannot "hear" logically. Anger, on both sides, obscures the truth that Teiresias possesses as an inborn gift (299).

Rather than providing a basis for a tragic flaw, this scene is the play's most dramatic enactment to this point of the tragedy of knowledge: truth is trapped in illusion and in the disturbances of language and emotion. There is also an implicit contrast between divine and human knowledge. Oedipus boasts of having saved Thebes by the human skill that solved the riddle, while the prophet of the god could do nothing (390). But he asserts this claim to human knowledge just as his own ignorance has become clearest to us. When Teiresias says "Apollo," Oedipus replies with his accusation of "Creon" (377–78). The prophet looks toward the god whom he serves, the king toward the human realm and human motives that he can understand. Moments before Teiresias's appearance Oedipus had cautioned against forcing the gods to speak when they are unwilling (280–81), yet he does just this in pressing Teiresias, their mouthpiece. When the gods do speak, through Teiresias, Oedipus is unable to hear what they say.

With Teiresias there enters onstage something beyond the limits of human knowledge. Despite his all-too-human irritability, he possesses a vision that extends into both the buried past and the dark future. As his prophecy hints, he is also a foreshadowing of what Oedipus will become (419, 454–56), but whereas these paradoxical collocations of sight and blindness, strength and weakness, are overt in Teiresias, they are still hidden in Oedipus.

Oedipus here resembles the Creon of the earlier *Antigone*: a ruler who denies the prophet's insight into sacred things and denigrates his vision by imputing to him merely secular motives (*Antigone*, 1033–63). But unlike Creon Oedipus is to evolve into a seer like Teiresias. In the later play, *Oedipus at Colonus*, Oedipus will be from the start the Teiresias figure that he is in the process of becoming here.

The clash between human and divine knowledge in this scene takes the form of the contrast between riddles and oracles, the two modes of knowledge that most sharply separate Oedipus and Teiresias. If Oedipus claims that the Sphinx's riddle needed a "prophecy" that Teiresias lacked (394), Teiresias gives Oedipus an oracle that poses a riddle: "How everything you say is too riddling and obscure," Oedipus complains after Teiresias foretells his horrible future (439). The oracle is a riddle that Oedipus cannot solve, as the chorus implies when it tries to intercede: "To us Teiresias' words seem to have been spoken in anger, and yours too, Oedipus. Of such words we have no need, but rather how best to consider *solving the prophecies* of the god" (404–7; my italics). Fair to both sides, the chorus perceives the anger in Teiresias as well as in Oedipus. What they cannot see is that this very anger is in fact helping to solve the god's prophecies—that is, to bring out the hidden truth of who Oedipus is.

The scene with Teiresias does advance the plot in one important respect: for the first time it raises the question of Oedipus's origins. "Do you know where you are?" asks Teiresias in the simplest possible language, just five monosyllables in the Greek (415). For the moment, the issue passes Oedipus by: the point is lost in the long list of mysterious horrors that Teiresias now utters and that Oedipus presumably regards as angry ranting (408–28). But a single word catches his attention in the line-by-line exchange immediately after. He dismisses Teiresias's doom-saying as "silly words," but Teiresias throws the insult back at him:

> Teiresias: Yes, silly, as you think, but full of understanding about the parents who begot you.
> Oedipus: What parents? Wait. What parents gave birth to me?
> Teiresias: This day will give birth to you—and will destroy you too.
> Oedipus: Very riddling all that you say, and all unclear.
> Teiresias: Are you not best at finding out such things as these?
> Oedipus: You insult me in just these things where you will find me great.
> Teiresias: Yet it is just this fortune (*tyche*) that has destroyed you.
> (435–42)

The passage is dense with ironies that echo throughout the play: the chance/mischance that makes Oedipus both "great" and small (1080–85); the motif of the single day, with its further associations of the precariousness of mortality; the mystery of Oedipus's origins; and the coexistence of his deep intelligence and his ignorance about the riddle of his past. Oedipus has directed all his formidable energy and intelligence at the search for Laius's killer. Except for his momentary distraction by Teiresias's word "parents," his thoughts are far from his own past.

107

This passage also shows how oracle and riddle complement one another as the two sides of Oedipus's tragic situation. The riddle points to his success and intelligence in saving Thebes and winning his high position. The oracle reveals his helplessness and ignorance before the larger powers that surround his life. In the prologue the priest had said that Oedipus had solved the riddle "by the help of a god" (38). Answering Teiresias, Oedipus claims the superior power of his purely human knowledge. Your prophecy, he says in effect, could not solve the riddle when my own intelligence did, "without the help of any god" (394–98). But, as we have seen, Teiresias's prophetic language is a riddle of another kind (439), deeper than that of the Sphinx.

Sophocles has been taking risks in this scene, but he pushes the tensions even further in Teiresias's parting shot, his final prophecy to Oedipus:

> . . . A stranger,
> you may think, who lives among you,
> he soon will be revealed a native Theban
> but he will take no joy in the revelation.
> Blind who now has eyes, beggar who now is rich,
> he will grope his way toward a foreign
> soil, a stick tapping before him step by step.
> Revealed at last, brother and father both
> to the children he embraces, to his mother
> son and husband both—he sowed the loins
> his father sowed, he spilled his father's blood!
> (Fagles's translation, 452–60)

How could Oedipus, famous riddle-solver, not grasp the truth when it is spoken so clearly? Teiresias's language is obscure, of course, as oracular language tends to be, and Oedipus also has the pressure of the city's crisis distracting him. Another answer is to suppose that Oedipus exits into the palace after he orders Teiresias's attendant to lead the old prophet away (445–46). In that case Teiresias would speak his prophecy to a retreating figure who does not hear him.[4] We have little solid evidence for Sophocles' staging, and this arrangement is possible. Dramatically, however, the tension is more effective if Oedipus remains onstage. In this way the horror of the prophet's uncanny knowledge stands in an even more powerful contrast with Oedipus's rationality, as Teiresias's closing two lines suggest: "Go inside and *reckon* these things up; and if you catch me as one who's false, then say that my *intelligence* in prophecy is nil" (461–62; my italics). Either way it is staged, the scene is a powerful visual enactment of the clash between human and divine knowledge.

It is characteristic of Sophocles' art that a formal symmetry contains and controls all these heated emotions. Teiresias exits with the same word with which he began, "intelligence" or "understanding" (*phronein*, ll. 462, 316). He is "the only man in whom truth is innate," the chorus tells Oedipus as the prophet enters (299). "Consider if you find me false," Teiresias says as he leaves (461). The echoes keep the intellectual themes in the foreground.

The scene has still another function in the progression of the action. Oedipus does not entirely forget Teiresias's words; he remembers them during Jocasta's more detailed account of the past: "I am in fearful despair that the prophet might have vision," he cries at that point (747), harking back to the metaphors of sight for knowledge and blindness for ignorance that play about his meeting with Teiresias. Thus the vagueness and horror of Teiresias's statement prepare us for his growing anxieties later and help us to feel them, too, as this incredible, nightmarish prophecy by an angry old man turns out to be fact.

FIRST STASIMON (SECOND CHORAL ODE)

The power of Teiresias's prophecy is kept alive in the choral ode (the first stasimon) that immediately follows his exit (463–512). Reacting to Teiresias's pronouncement, the chorus combines puzzlement about the killer's identity with confidence in the radiant truth of Delphic prophecy. The ode invites us to connect the Delphic oracle given to Creon with what we have just heard from Teiresias, and in this way it opens further speculation on the interconnections among all the oracles in the background and thereby also deepens the rift between human and divine knowledge. At the same time it shows the city's deep confidence in Oedipus and its belief in his innocence. After all, Teiresias, though a prophet, is a

109

mortal man, while Zeus and Apollo are gods, and so (the elders imply) Teiresias could be wrong (489–506). Remembering again how their king saved the city by defeating the Sphinx, they conclude with their faith in Oedipus unshaken (504–11).

As is often true in Sophocles' plays, however, the ode points to other meanings. "Delphi's prophetic rock" and the snowy peak of Parnassus (the mountain on which Delphi stands) at the beginning of the first strophe and antistrophe, respectively (463–64, 473–75), form part of a pattern that associates the mountains with the unknown, demonic world beyond human knowledge. Cithaeron was the mountain where Oedipus was exposed to die as an infant. Teiresias had mentioned it ominously (421), and it will recur powerfully later. Delphi, which (as the chorus sings) holds the "mid-navel of the earth" (480), contrasts with the wild landscape above it, where the unknown killer wanders, among "savage woods and caves, [as] the bull of the rocks" (477). These images of remote wilderness will, at the end of the play, fit Oedipus the polluted outcast who asks to be expelled to Mount Cithaeron (1451ff; see also 1391ff, 1088). When the chorus declares that "Apollo, son of Zeus, is leaping armed upon" the killer, they take up a metaphor that Oedipus had used of Laius's death (263) and that he will use again of himself when the horrible truth emerges (1311). This "leaping" of a god, like the mountains and the bull, mysteriously combines bestiality and divinity and weaves the thread of divine causation into the human action of investigation and discovery.

SECOND EPISODE

After the references to the remote gods in the scene with Teiresias and the chorus, the play moves back to human behavior and politics with the return of Creon in the second episode. He enters with an address to Thebes's "citizens" and a reference to Oedipus with his full title, "the ruler Oedipus" (*ton tyrannon Oedipoun* [513–14]). This is a very different entrance from Creon's first appearance, for Oedipus has lost no time in making known his suspicions. Dramatically, the scene keeps our attention directed away from Oedipus's own history and prevents the revelation of the truth from coming too soon. Sophocles wants to delay discovery in the play and to stimulate expectation, and the scene with Creon accomplishes both admirably.

Instead of the mysterious thought-world of the blind prophet and his terrible knowledge, we are on the familiar ground (familiar, at least, to an Athenian audience) of legal debate. This is a courtroom scene, and it unfolds entirely on the level of human motivation and behavior. Oedipus is angry, suspicious, and in control. He is determined to take all the necessary precautions against a conspiracy. His deduction is not unreasonable, given the circumstantial evidence. Creon is a likely successor to Oedipus; he and Teiresias knew each other long before Oedipus's arrival; and the idea of consulting Teiresias originated with Creon (288). The city's crisis would be a natural time for a coup d'état. Perhaps they even conspired in the past, too, to eliminate Laius and share the power but were prevented by Oedipus's arrival. In any case, as a ruler from outside, a "tyrant" rather than a "king" (514) Oedipus has reason to feel insecure. Not all of this reasoning is presented overtly in the play, nor is it all absolutely necessary, but this is the kind of deduction that an Athenian audience, thoroughly steeped in political machinations, might expect Oedipus to be making.

In contrast to Oedipus, with his impetuous energy, Creon is reasonable and even a little pedantic. He is cautious where Oedipus is rash—a difference to be reenacted in the final scene. He has good answers to Oedipus's accusations: Oedipus should verify the response he brought from Delphi and investigate any previous association between Creon and Teiresias. To Oedipus, however, this only sounds incriminating: he assumes that Creon has taken care to cover his tracks and that he is stalling for time. He knows, rightly, that a conspiracy could move quickly, especially at this time of crisis in the city, and that he too "must make [his] counterplot with speed" (619–20). Exile or death had been the cleansing prescribed by Delphi and endorsed by Oedipus, and Creon assumes that Oedipus will ask for the lighter penalty, but the king has decided differently: "Your death, not your exile, is what I want" (623).

This insistence on the death penalty, along with the emphasis on haste, suggests that Oedipus is veering toward the imperiousness of the bad ruler, the tyrant in the pejorative sense, like Creon in *Antigone*. Indeed, when Oedipus exclaims, "O city, city," Creon replies, "But I too and not you alone have a share in the city" (630), and the line recalls the debate between the autocratic Creon and his son Haemon in that earlier play. "There is no city that belongs to a single man," Haemon had told his father (*Antigone*, 737; see also *Oedipus Tyrannus*, 579).

At this impasse Jocasta enters from the palace. This is the first time since the opening scene that Sophocles stages a three-way exchange (four ways, with the chorus). Jocasta had been mentioned briefly in the previous scene of debate between Oedipus and Creon: "Oedipus: I will not be convicted as the killer. / Creon: What then, don't you hold my sister in marriage?" (576–77). That apparently fortuitous, though abrupt, transition from Oedipus as "killer" of Laius to Oedipus as having Jocasta "in marriage" seems innocent and natural in its context, but it now takes on a darker meaning when Jocasta enters and soon after describes the oracle that her child was to be "the killer of his father" (721).

Jocasta's opening words show at once her commanding presence and authority. Both Creon and Oedipus treat her with respect, although we may shudder a little at Creon's first line to her (639), which brings together the terms "sister of the same blood" and "Oedipus your husband," reminding us that husband is also of the same blood.[5] In any case she and the chorus of elders together persuade Oedipus to accept, reluctantly, Creon's oath of innocence. But the men do not part on good terms; Creon's parting shot, like Teiresias's in the previous scene, holds a warning for Oedipus, although this lies wholly in human terms, in Oedipus's character: "Such natures are rightly most painful for themselves to bear" (674–75). Oedipus is unforgiving: "Won't you leave me and get yourself away?" (677). This sharp parting will add to Oedipus's shame when Creon returns at the end.

The short scene that follows (679–702) repeats a now-familiar pattern: one character tries to elicit answers, and the respondent is reluctant to tell. The questioner is Jocasta, and the one who withholds information is Oedipus, evasive about Teiresias's accusation that he is Laius's killer. It is the reverse of the situation between Oedipus and Teiresias, and the situation will reverse again in the following scene, close to the discovery, when Oedipus presses Jocasta for more details and Jocasta begs him to stop (1056ff). She in fact uses the same entreaty, "by the gods," in both cases (698 and 1060; see also 326, 646, 1037, 1153).

When Oedipus does finally report Teiresias's words, Jocasta's reassurance that prophets have no skill anyway sets into motion another narrative pattern: the one who tries to bring relief in fact brings disaster. This pattern has already been at work in the oracle from Delphi and in the appearance of Teiresias, and it will occur again. Here, to prove that "the prophetic art" is worthless, Jocasta tells how Laius was killed by robbers, not by his own child, as the oracle foretold. This is the first report of this oracle in the play, and to it Jocasta adds the detail of the triple crossroads, which immediately electrifies Oedipus (707–27). In fact, she supplies him with several new facts: the oracle itself, her exposure of a child on the mountain after "yoking together its feet," and Laius's death at the "triple road." She also confirms the earlier tale of "robbers" as the murderers.

In all of Jocasta's narrative Oedipus picks up only the one phrase, about the "triple roads" (727). The situation resembles Oedipus's dialogue with Teiresias: the prophet's full accusation had little effect, but a single word ("parents") throws him into turmoil. For the first time we see the commanding power of the king falter. He will never again regain the confidence and composure of the opening scenes, although at the end he will find a strength of another kind.

9

Discovery and Reversal

JOCASTA AND OEDIPUS

The tale of Jocasta comes at approximately the halfway point of the play and is a turning point in the action. It causes an abrupt shift in Oedipus, from power, confidence, and control to uncertainty and fear. He continues to act rapidly and efficiently, but he is now on the defensive. More important, the direction of his search is completely changed, for he now begins to search not just for the killer of Laius but also for himself.

Creon's exit at line 677 encourages the one-on-one dialogue between the king and queen, although the chorus, in accordance with the conventions of Greek tragedy, remains on stage and even participates in the discussion (834–35). The scene is long (634–862) and is carefully balanced between the two crucial narratives about the past, first Jocasta's, then Oedipus's. Sophocles, unlike Euripides, is not concerned with domestic realism, and the dialogue between Oedipus and Jocasta remains formal and severe. She repeatedly addresses him as "lord" (697, 770, 852). Although there is nothing particularly domestic in their talk, this concerned, more or less private exchange between husband and wife evokes something of the marital bond between them and contrasts markedly with the more public, heated exchanges that Oedipus has just had with Teiresias and Creon. The quieter setting, too, helps refocus the action on Oedipus's recollection of his past.

By using Jocasta as the means to Oedipus's discovery of the truth, Sophocles gains the effect of a double tragedy, for Jocasta's

114

denial and recognition begin to parallel those of Oedipus himself. As we shall see, he also creates a double climax as the two protagonists come to their respective recognitions at different times. There is a tragic irony in the way in which Jocasta directs the action from the human to divine knowledge. She cites her oracle to disprove the validity of prophecy, and her skepticism about oracles continues into the next scene (see 977–83). But her story about Laius's oracle only sharpens the question of divine foreknowledge and the role, therefore, of some external force that governs human lives.

The irony of this reverse effect is conveyed in a verbal play that is difficult to translate into English. Jocasta would disprove the validity of Laius's oracle about his child with the explanation, "As the rumor (*phatis*) is, strangers, robbers, killed Laius at the triple roads" (715–16). Her term for "rumor" here, *phatis*, also means "oracle" and is so used regularly throughout the play. Thus her words can also mean something like, "He died *as the oracle said he would*," which is the exact opposite of what she intended to say. It remains one of the mysterious coincidences working in the play that she chooses just this moment to tell of a past with which she has lived for so many years. Here too the motif of chance or fortune, *tyche*, is important.

Under the impact of Jocasta's revelation, Oedipus, so concerned with Thebes's present crisis, begins to look away to the past, indeed to his own past, not in Thebes but in Corinth, at Delphi, and the "triple road" between these three cities. He now tells his own story, the foil to Jocasta's. It is a critical narrative, and we must attend to it carefully. Sophocles has withheld it until this crucial point at the center of the play so that we will listen to it with the suspense and horror that Jocasta's accounts of the deaths of both her child and Laius have aroused.

Telling the story of his life, Oedipus begins, of course, with his parents: his father was Polybus of Corinth, his mother Merope of Doris (774–75). It is the most natural of beginnings, but we know how deeply flawed even this "innocent" statement is. What Oedipus takes to be the least problematic part of his tale will soon become his most anxious point of inquiry. Indeed, he goes on to tell how he went to Delphi to ask about his parents. Apollo's reply was terrifying, and Oedipus reports it in the first person: "I must have intercourse with my mother and show to men a race unendurable to

look upon, and I will be the killer of the father who begot me"
(791–93). This is the third and last of the oracles mentioned in the
play, the other two having been Creon's report from Delphi and
Jocasta's account of the oracle given to Laius. But this is the first
time we hear of an oracle given directly from the god to the person
for whom it is intended (788ff). Whereas Jocasta had tried to blunt
the force of the address from the god ("not from Apollo himself but
from his servants" [711–12]), Oedipus's account makes us feel the
awe of encountering the divine voice, and he tells us he at once fled
Corinth in terror.

Oedipus still does not see any connection among the three oracles, for neither of the two previously mentioned had said anything
about incest. His immediate concern is that he may be Laius's killer
and therefore subject to the terrible curse that he pronounced
against this person earlier. This concern is uppermost in his mind
as he tells of his fatal meeting at the crossroads. It is a story
emblematic of Oedipus's destiny as a hero who supplants his father
in every way, and it uses the motif of walking as a symbol of a journey through life, a journey marked by tragedy and bloodshed.

A young man on foot is attempting to advance on his path, but
his way is blocked by an older man, bearing all the trappings of
power and wealth. The "old man" strikes just as he "sees" the
younger "trying to pass by his chariot," that is, as the youth tries to
make his way beyond this blocking figure on the road of life. It is a
cruel blow, with a double-pointed ox-goad, aimed at the head, and
Oedipus struck back in anger (800–813).

Oedipus's account stresses the deliberate aggressiveness of the
older man: he is the one who "sees," "aims" his blow, and "comes
down with it" on the head of Oedipus (807–9). The active verbs of
this man's attack are followed by the passive verbs of his fall, as he
is "struck" and "rolled out" of the chariot (811–12). Oedipus evokes
the scene in only five lines, with a few rapid, specific details.
Though it happened some 20 years before, it is as fresh as if it were
yesterday, and he tells most of it in the present tense. The five
verses of Laius's actions, in the third person, are framed by
Oedipus's two simple, direct first-person statements, both in the
historical present tense: "I strike in anger" (807) and "I kill them all"
(813).[1]

"I killed them all," Oedipus says, quite simply, but Laius struck first, and so to strike back was justifiable homicide. Was it justifiable to kill the others, or was that too in self-defense? Oedipus's concern is not with the legal problems; instead, he worries about the curse that he himself pronounced on the killer, the cause of the plague, and about the added pollution of being married to the wife of the man he killed (813–33). As he views the consequences of his act from his present distance, he shifts abruptly from the vivid narrative style to more abstract language. If that "stranger" whom he killed "has any relation of kinship with Laius," he says, "then who is more wretched, who more hateful to the gods than I?" (813–16). Still holding to a shred of hope, he is careful to describe the stranger in a noncommittal, cautious way, but his word "kinship" evokes his still hidden family connections and here contrasts ironically with "stranger," which can refer to both Oedipus and Laius, who are of course not strangers but son and father.

If Oedipus is Laius's killer, he must go into exile to free Thebes from the plague and fulfill his own curse. But because of his oracle he cannot go back to Corinth and his "parents," for the oracle had foretold that he would commit incest and parricide (825–27). The levels of Oedipus's ignorance compound the ironies, for of course he has already committed the crimes foretold in the oracle. When he says that he will not be permitted to "see my people" (824) he ironically foreshadows his future blindness. When he speaks of Polybus as "the father who *nurtured* and *begot* me," his reversal of the normal biological order contains the hidden truth that Polybus only nurtured him. We also recall the terms of the oracle as Oedipus first gave it, that he "will be the killer of the father *who begot me*" (792). Sophocles makes the oracle prove to be true with a bitter literalness: Oedipus has two fathers, Laius and Polybus, and he kills the one who begot him. This is also the father who, because of his own oracle, did *not* nurture him.

The clustering of the oracles at this point works closely with the gradual emergence of powers beyond human control. When Oedipus refers to the "cruel divinity" (*daimon*, 828) that has guided his life and its luck, he harks back to his statement just before (816), that he had a "hostile daimon" over his life. The man who had seemed so much in control now looks increasingly toward strange, supernatural forces that seem to surround him. *Daimon*, his word in lines 816 and 828, is the most general term for "divinity," and Oedipus will use it again after the discovery and self-blinding: "O daimon, where you leapt forth" (1311). Then he will have learned how cruel that daimon has been and how closely it is connected with the role of Apollo (see 1329ff).

Everything now turns on the question of one killer or many, and Oedipus presents this as a problem of calculation: if the Herdsman, the sole witness, "still declares the same *number*, then I didn't kill him, for one would not be equal to many" (843–45). Oedipus is still the man of reason and reckoning. But his logic of noncontradiction, "one would not equal many," will not work in the strange world opening before him, where he is the most tragic paradox of all, the figure who in fact is one and many simultaneously. The play rings many changes on the ironies of counting, particularly in Teiresias's prophetic vision of the coexisting opposites in Oedipus, which he ended with the taunt, "Go inside and *calculate* these things" (460–61).

Oedipus, though fearful, is still logical, but Jocasta becomes more desperate. She relies not so much on logic as on the irrelevant argument that the witness cannot take back what he once declared before the whole city (849–50). Then she falls back on the oracle to Laius that initially provoked all the terror. Even if the Herdsman should change his story, she says, there is still the oracle that Laius "must die at the hands of my child; and yet that unfortunate child didn't kill him but himself perished first" (854–57). She has almost stumbled on the truth, but she immediately veers away to the wrong conclusion.

As Oedipus clings to rational calculation and the logic of non-contradiction (one cannot be equal to many), Jocasta clings to the denial of oracles—a denial that only reveals how deeply involved she remains with the oracle of Laius's death and her own "dead" child.[2] Nevertheless, the exposed child still has a kind of life for her, as she refers to him as "that unfortunate one" (855), and she will repeat that term as the "last thing" she has to call Oedipus in her horrified recognition of the truth at the end of the next scene. The present scene ends with Oedipus, characteristically, pressing on for more evidence and demanding to see the Herdsman-witness.

THE SECOND STASIMON (THIRD CHORAL ODE)

The choral ode that follows the scene with Jocasta and Oedipus (863–910) allows time for the Herdsman's arrival, but it has many other functions. It is a complex poem and one of the most controversial in Sophocles' work. On the surface it is a prayer for piety, justice, and a world of moral clarity where the evil are punished and the oracles are a valid sign of the gods' presence in human affairs. More profoundly, it shows the people's attitude toward the oracles, and therefore toward the gods and the divine order generally, polarized between a belief in divine governance (see especially 898–910) and a belief that everything in life is random, that it all happens by chance. This is the position that Jocasta will enunciate at the beginning of the next scene. Thus the ode is to be seen not simply as a statement of pious belief by a serene Sophocles demonstrating divine justice, but rather as a meeting point of opposite ways of trying to make sense of random suffering. Jocasta will die in her anguished vision of a random or irrational world order that has doomed her and those she loves to terrible suffering; the voices of the chorus here provide a counterstatement: they want to believe in a moral order emanating from the gods, but they speak in general terms that do not fit the present circumstances at every point.

The first strophe invokes the laws in the heavens, a timeless, ageless order fathered by the gods, not born from mortal nature (856ff). This incorruptible law of the gods, however, seems remote from humankind. Eternal, celestial, and elusive, it is at the furthest possible remove from the tangled, impure, incestuous origins of Oedipus that are so much involved with "fathers," "birth," and "begetting," all prominent words in this passage. The adjective "high-footed" that describes the Olympian laws (in the sense of "lofty" or "on high") suggests a tragic contrast in this distance, for it reminds us of the recurrent image of feet in the play and especially of "Oedi-pous," whose feet keep him very much on earth and among the mortal woes of birth and generation.

The antistrophe warns, "Insulting violence [*hybris*] begets the tyrant," and it continues with warnings about the man of excess who is lifted too high and then cast down to earth "with useless foot" (878)—that is, injured and impotent. Does "tyrant" here mean

119

only "ruler," as it usually does in the play, or does it mean "tyrant" in the pejorative sense, which is certainly possible in this period? And is the chorus referring to Oedipus or to evil men in general and especially to the still-unknown killer? The problem is difficult, but we should not jump to the conclusion that the ode is just an attack on Oedipus for his "tragic flaw." Oedipus has shown anger but not really *hybris*—violence—or injustice, and the chorus's attitude toward him has been consistently favorable. At most, this section of the ode reflects the discrepancy between the terrible fate that the oracles seem to be accumulating for Oedipus and the basic decency and just behavior of his life and rule.

What the ode brings out most poignantly is the gap between the timeless laws of remote Olympus and the struggles of men on earth to understand the ways of the gods and to make moral sense of their lives. And yet the chorus, as a voice of civic concern and ordinary morality, desperately wants the world to make sense and wants to believe in the established religious institutions, the worship of the gods in rituals like choral dance and the oracles.

The opening of the ode, with its reference to Olympus and the divine laws "in the celestial ether," recalls the high summit of "snowy Parnassus" in the previous ode, from which the first oracle "flashed forth" to point the way to healing Thebes's plague (473–76). These two high mountains of truth, light, and purity, Parnassus and Olympus, serve as symbols of the remoteness and inscrutability of divine will. Against them stand the earth of Thebes and the local Theban mountain, Cithaeron, connected with Oedipus's past and his future, and with mortal generation, birth, impurity, and suffering. As more oracles have emerged, that divine will is far less clear; as the end of the ode implies, the chorus is caught between wanting to see the authority of the gods maintained and not wanting to see the suffering that the truth of those oracles now implies.

The ode's opening image of divine laws engendered outside of time also reminds us that the oracles, in the timeless perspective of the gods, have already been fulfilled. The gods have seen them as both going to happen and having already happened. The next scene shows the protagonists caught in time, trying to unravel the mysteries of their past to understand what they are in the present. To be free of time, like the gods, is also to be free of its tragic patterns of birth, change, generation, memory and forgetting (see 870 and 904), and death.

THIRD EPISODE

The ode's broad perspectives on the distance between men and gods contrast with the immediate anxieties of the two following scenes (911–1085, 1110–1185), which are the climax of the play as the horrifying truth of Oedipus's past emerges into the light. Here, as Aristotle observed, the discovery or recognition (*anagnorisis*) brings about the reversal (peripety, *peripeteia*), and this coincidence, in Aristotle's view, makes for the best kind of tragedy (*Poetics*, 11.1452a32).

In keeping with Sophocles' sense of form, the two scenes are symmetrical. In each a new character enters: first the Messenger from Corinth, then the Herdsman. Each ends in a powerful discovery: the first with Jocasta's cry at her recognition of the truth (1072–73), the second with Oedipus's similar discovery and outcry (1182; see also 1071). The previous scene had ended with Oedipus's energetic summoning of the Herdsman (859–62), and it is his appearance that we expect. Instead, a new and hitherto unmentioned figure from Corinth delays the recognition for Oedipus, but he gives Jocasta enough information for her to piece together that part of the truth that has most concerned her, the identity of the child she and Laius exposed at its birth.

The choral ode of hope and confidence that separates the two scenes (1086–1109) not only heightens the suspense but also creates what is perhaps the play's most powerful dramatic irony, the last and greatest contrast between illusion and truth. The contrast is also enacted visually in the staging. Jocasta exits in full, tragic knowledge; Oedipus continues on the stage in his misguided optimism. Their roles are also the reverse of that of the previous scene, where he had been the fearful one and she had maintained optimism and hope.

Just before the Messenger's entrance, as we have noted, the chorus sang of the honor due to Apollo and his oracles. Jocasta's entrance with wreathes and incense suggests a frightened change

121

from her previous skepticism and also harks back to the play's opening rituals of supplication. Her entrance marks a kind of second beginning, but its echo of the first scene also provides a measure of the change of mood. Instead of being confidently in control, Oedipus is fearful and despondent; instead of being the one to be supplicated, supplication is offered on his behalf. "We are all in fear," Jocasta explains, "seeing him panic-stricken, as one would fear for the pilot of a ship" (922–23). The familiar metaphor of the ship of state harks back to the nautical metaphors of earlier scenes, where Oedipus's rule is compared to piloting a sea-tossed vessel (23–24, 694–96), but now not the ship but the pilot himself is in trouble. In the first ode the chorus had described itself, collectively, as "trembling with fear" (155); in this scene Oedipus, in his anxiety about the oracles, is twice described as "trembling" (947, 1014).

Sophocles may well have invented the entire episode of the Corinthian Messenger. In any case, it is a brilliant stroke not only thus to delay the final discovery but also to juxtapose the innocent and peaceful death of Polybus with the violent death of Laius. With the heightened mood of anxiety in Jocasta, we might expect a messenger's speech that will reveal all. The end of the previous scene, as we have noted, led us to expect the Herdsman, who would, of course, bring the investigation to its horrible conclusion. Instead, the Messenger's entrance is the prelude to two scenes of intense question-and-answer dialogue. The effect is to create suspense and to make the recognition emerge from Oedipus's determination to find the truth. The author of a recent commentary on the play writes, "With the possible exception of some scenes in Homer, the next 300 lines constitute the finest achievement in Greek poetic technique to have survived to our era."[3]

The scene carries double meanings and verbal ironies to a new pitch. The Messenger begins with a play on Oedipus's name and on the Greek phrase "know where" (*oida pou*), and the chorus in reply points out Jocasta as "Oedipus's wife and mother—of his children" (924–26, 928). There is a further irony in the situation: the Messenger seems to be savoring Oedipus's happiness and success, in part because (as we learn later) he rescued him from death and in part because he expects to increase that happiness by bringing what he assumes to be good news from Corinth and thus to win a handsome reward (1006). Instead, every piece of news, every propitious word, will turn to its exact opposite.

If the preceeding ode suggested that the human situation is tragic because it is caught in time, this scene reveals the tragic situation of being caught in language. The ambiguities of speech both result from and in turn feed the illusions in which these lives are enmeshed. The power of speech that Sophocles' contemporaries regarded as one of man's unique gifts, the basis of the legal and political system of the Athenian democracy, is here shown to be a source of the deepest error. Teiresias, as we have seen, has "truth" as an inborn gift, but when he puts it into human language he is accused of lies (see 461). In the present scene the Messenger also asserts his claim to truth ("If I do not speak the truth I deserve death" [944]), but this truth is dreadfully entangled with the errors surrounding basic kinship terms like *father* and *mother* and even the name of the king of the land.

The Messenger announces the death of King Polybus, and Jocasta, who seems almost maternally solicitous of Oedipus's moods, seizes on the words as she had seized on the "one robber" in the Herdsman's original story. The oracles are worthless, she cries joyfully, since Polybus died "by chance" and not at his son Oedipus's hand (946–49). But chance, as always in the play, proves far from helpful.

Oedipus arrives with the "speed" that Jocasta had recommended (945) and shares Jocasta's joy at the death of his "father" and her relief that the oracle of his parricide and incest cannot come true (950–87). Ironically, his joy in having escaped the oracle echoes the words of Teiresias who foretold its fulfillment. Oedipus says,

> Why should one look
> to the birds screaming overhead? They prophesied
> that I should kill my father! But he's *dead*,
> *and hidden deep in earth*
> (Grene's translation, 965–68; my italics)

Teiresias had said, "Do you know who your parents are? Unknowing / you are an enemy to kith and kin / *in death, beneath the earth and in this life*" (Grene's translation, 414–17; my italics). In his conflict with Teiresias Oedipus had scornfully dismissed prophecy and the reading of bird-signs (398); here he repeats that confidence in purely human knowledge, only to demonstrate how ill-founded such confidence is.

When Oedipus expresses continuing anxiety about the other part of the oracle, incest with his mother, Jocasta reassures him by generalizing enthusiastically on the principle of "randomness" or chance in human life:

> Why should man fear since chance rules everything
> for him, and he can clearly foreknow nothing?
> Best to live randomly, as one can, unthinkingly.
> As to your mother's marriage bed,—don't fear it.
> Before this, in dreams too, as well as oracles,
> many a man has lain with his own mother.
> But he to whom such things are nothing bears
> his life most easily.
>
> (Grene's translation [slightly modified], 977–83)

She is urging that we live our days one at a time, without concern with a divine plan or supernatural direction or meaning for our life. Jocasta is not necessarily being impious here, but in her release from the catastrophe hanging over her and Oedipus, she pulls back gladly to a nontragic attitude of enjoying life. Why should one's life, after all, have some awful shape behind it? Why is it that decent people cannot live out happy, ordinary lives, taking each day as it comes? But this eagerness to deny the power of oracles also comes from a woman who saw her newly born son sacrificed to the fear of an oracle.

Oedipus mentions his continuing fear of the other part of his oracle, incest with his mother, and this alerts the Messenger. He had let Jocasta's earlier reference to Polybus being Oedipus's father go by in line 955, but he becomes interested in Oedipus's supposed "fear of his mother" (988–89), and this in turn leads him to announce that Polybus and his wife are not really Oedipus's parents. The effect of this statement is analogous to the first scene of revelation, in which Jocasta's account of her oracle led to the chance mention of the triple road.

Oedipus now resumes his earlier role as the keen investigator, but his curiosity about himself, which had flashed into his mind briefly at Teiresias's reference to his parents (437), has now obliterated his search for Laius's killer. The Messenger's negative fact ("Polybus is no kin to you" [1016]) leads to the next electrifying piece of positive information, "I found you in Cithaeron's glades" (1026).[4] The name of the mountain had been pronounced only once before in the play, in Teiresias's prophecy, "What [part of] Cithaeron will not echo with your cries" (421), and we now see a pattern beginning to take shape that links the origins of Oedipus's life with its tragic character.

When the Messenger calls himself Oedipus's "savior," having "released" him from the bonds that "pierced his feet" (1030–34), he repeats the pattern of reversals in which "saving" and "release" produce the opposite effect (see 921, 1003). This is the first specific mention of piercing the feet; Jocasta had called them "yoked" in her story (718)—a vaguer and gentler description, but she is standing by in silence, hearing everything and fitting it all together. Because the actors wore masks, there would have been no change of facial expression to indicate that she has recognized the truth, but the actor could have signalled this with a gesture like a start of horror.

The Messenger's mention of the pierced feet, however, does elicit a response from Oedipus, the cry *oimoi* ("alas"). "Why," he asks, "do you mention that old suffering?" (1033). The abrupt cry creates another moment of suspense. Has Oedipus in fact seen the truth? If he pieces the fragments together now, the recognition would be upon us. Once more Sophocles has pushed the dramatic tension to the furthest possible point.

The Messenger, however, has more to tell, and Oedipus is eager for the details. He takes Oedipus back to that buried childhood:

> Oedipus: Terrible the insult that I received from my swaddling clothes.
> Messenger: So that you were named who you are from that chance.
> Oedipus: Oh, in the gods' name, was it from my mother or father? Tell me!
> Messenger: I don't know. The giver knows this better than I.
> Oedipus: Did you then take me from someone else and find me by chance?
> Messenger: No; another, a herdsman, gave you to me. (1035–40)

Trying to pierce the darkness of that mysterious time of his birth, Oedipus seems to be drawing on old, buried memories: the "old hurt" to his feet, the curiosity about his name, and the "insult" from his "swaddling clothes" that recalls the insult about his birth with which he was taunted at Thebes long ago (1035 and 784). In place of the normal care of a baby's "swaddling clothes" he received only the pierced feet that gave him his name, "swollen foot" (*oidein*, "to swell," and *pous*, "foot"). By refusing him a name, his parents also refused him a normal human identity; they condemned him to a social as well as a biological death. In the untranslatable pun of line 1038, "the-giver-knows" (*oid' ho dous*) names *Oidipous*.[5]

So far, the scene has concentrated on the two male interlocutors. Now, as the tension relaxes slightly, the chorus contributes another piece of the puzzle: the "giver" of Oedipus to the Messenger seems to be the same Herdsman/escort/witness who has already been summoned (1047–53). This last bit of information leads Oedipus back to Jocasta, who has been standing by in silence during the whole interrogation. When he had first entered, in line 950, he had addressed her by name (the only time in the play) and with a mixture of dignity and affection, "My dearest wife, Jocasta." Now he is clipped and colloquial: "Wife, do you recall that man—the one we just sent after? Is he the one whom this man here means?" (1054–55). Jocasta stalls for time, repeats the question, and tries to distract him: "Pay no attention to what was said; make no mention of it; it would all be in vain" (1056–57). Her language is elliptical and cryptic, as it must be, for we see that she has recognized the truth. Her only hope is to persuade Oedipus to stop. Her advice, especially the phrase "it would be all in vain" or "all to no purpose," recalls her earlier statement about "living at random." In fact her word for "mention" (1057) also means "remember," so that there are implications of old memories—old oracles, old actions—coming fearfully alive, as they will come alive for her in the last words she utters in life, as reported by the Second Messenger later, when she again speaks of "mentioning/memory" (1246).

Oedipus removes all hope and dooms himself, and her too, with his predictable refusal: "This cannot be; there is no way for me to take such tokens and not show forth my birth" (1058–59). His word "tokens" or "signs" (*semeia*) belongs to the myth of the foundling. An abandoned baby frequently has such tokens left with him, as in the story of Ion in Euripides' *Ion* and in a number of folklore versions of the Oedipus myth. In fairy tales of this type such tokens prove the child to be of princely or divine birth and confirm his right to the kingdom. In Oedipus's case the "tokens" are the scars on his feet that in one way prove his royal birth but in another way undo his kingship.

The next moments are among the most anguished of the play. Oedipus and Jocasta have hitherto been subject to the same errors and illusions, and Jocasta has supported Oedipus in his fears and impatience, in the ups and downs of hope or worry. Now their paths diverge, and Oedipus will face the rest of his suffering alone. He, the hunter and searcher, cannot be stopped by her pleas. Her last words to him are those of a mother and wife both. She knows his nature and knows, too, that her desperate cries will have no effect, but she still makes a last attempt to save him.

"If you care for your own life," she begs him, "don't search this out. My disease is enough" (1060–61). This is almost her last utterance in the play, and her metaphor of "disease" contains a full recognition of what their life together now means. It not only takes up the literal disease of the plague but also reveals its source in the diseaselike pollution that spreads out like an infection from the house of Oedipus—the "house" to which the Messenger at his entrance promised "good things" (934). "I well know that you are diseased," Oedipus had said to the suppliants compassionately in the opening scene of the play, "but there is none of you who bears this disease equally with me" (59–61). The full truth of Oedipus's unique place in this disease is now becoming clear.

The whole of this discovery scene has taken us closer than ever to the mystery of Oedipus's name. "Named *who you are* from that chance" (1036), the Messenger had said. "May you never know *who you are*" (1068), Jocasta now cries. And her last words of the scene are also a final naming: "Unfortunate—this is the last address I have for you—nothing else ever again" (1071–72). The mother who gave him no name at his birth now renames him in his terrible maturity, "Unfortunate." It is the same term that she used for her doomed infant in the previous scene, in her attempt to show that oracles do not come true (855).

The chorus is alarmed at her distraught, silent exit (1073–75), which, like that of Deianeira in *Trachinian Women* and Eurydice in

Antigone, forebodes suicide. Oedipus, however, is blinded by his hope of discovering his parents. Once more he is the eager quester for truth. Let her go, he says, to "rejoice in her rich birth" (1070). He means that she can still take pleasure in her royal ancestry, whatever his birth may be; but the phrase also means "rich kinship" and so alludes to the over-rich kinship of the incestuous union. Calling himself a "child of chance" (1080), Oedipus is sure that he "will not be dishonored" by being proved the child of a slave. The choral ode that follows takes up his confident mood with speculations in the opposite direction, that he may be the child of a god. In fact, however, chance and time, which Oedipus regards as his allies ("the months my kindred" [1082]), have worked together to produce a life of total "dishonor."

THIRD STASIMON (FOURTH CHORAL ODE)

Carried along by Oedipus's mood of elation, the chorus sings an ode (the third stasimon) that depicts a mountain world of nymphs and Pan, shepherds and bacchants. Dionysus, whom the first ode invoked against the plague, now reappears in a more joyful setting. So do all the major mountains of Greece, with Cithaeron prominent among them, to be honored as Oedipus's "fatherland and nurse and mother" (1092). "Nurse" and "mother" are in the reverse of the biological order, as were the analogous terms on the father's side when Oedipus first spoke of Polybus who "nurtured and begot me" (827). This error about his mother, who is now very much in our minds after Jocasta's sudden departure, parallels the mistake about his father. The truth about both parents will soon make Oedipus curse Cithaeron (1451–54).

This ode is almost the reverse of the previous one, both in mood and content. The previous ode emphasized the gap between god and mortal and the remoteness of the gods on Olympus. The almost hysterical joy of the present ode brings the gods close to men and gives semidivine status to a doomed mortal. The god of the previous ode was an unnamed power (872, 881), pure and remote, the defender of timeless laws in an ageless world free of procreation and birth. The gods of this ode are jolly, playful beings who cavort with mountain nymphs (1099–1100), "join in their sport" (1109), and beget mortal children, one of whom is supposedly Oedipus. In turning away from the tragic realities of Oedipus's birth, the chorus also turns away from the austere vision of "god" in the previous ode to the playful multiplicity of specific, named gods in their fully anthropomorphic, sensual aspects. By mythicizing both the gods and Oedipus's birth, they distort the truth of both.

FIFTH EPISODE

With this joyful song still in our ears, we see the long-awaited Herdsman enter the orchestra. Herdsmen are rude and rustic workers and slaves, and this old man, come from the hills and the company of his beasts, forms a sharp contrast to the nymphs and playful gods of the ode. He brings us back to reality in more ways than one. The chorus quickly identifies him as "Laius's trusty herdsman," and the Messenger also names him as the man of whom he has been speaking (1117–20). The Herdsman at first says little, only a line at a time, but the Messenger, ever eager to volunteer details in what he thinks is a helpful and profitable course, reminds him of that remote time when the two of them tended sheep together on Cithaeron (1132–40).

This is the only departure from line-by-line repartee in the scene, and it depicts an almost bucolic serenity in the herdsmen's seasonal rhythms, "from spring to winter, six-month seasons," as they make their regular shift from summer to winter pasture (1136–39). The scene's workaday routine is a pendant to the mythically colored mountain landscape of the previous ode, and it offers a momentary respite from the looming horror. Its quiet, untragic view of time in the dull life of shepherds also sets off, by contrast, Oedipus's measuring and calculating of critical dates and the moment-by-moment tension of the present scene.

"You speak the truth, although from a long time ago," the Herdsman says, as he acknowledges the Messenger's recollection of events (1141). "Truth from a long time ago" seems like an ordinary line, but it crystallizes what is happening onstage: the process whereby truth—the truth that Teiresias had by inborn nature—is gradually forced out of its covering of time. The scattered bits of the past now fit into the pattern that had been shrouded in falsehood for so long.

The Messenger, happy to do his new king a service, as he thinks it, emphatically identifies the Herdsman, but the latter tries to shut him up: "Go to perdition, won't you! Won't you keep silent?" (1146). The outcry in the first half of the line holds one of those small ironies in Sophocles' use of colloquial speech, for it exactly echoes Oedipus's cry when Teiresias pronounced him the killer of Laius and the source of the pollution: "Is it endurable to hear such things from this man here? *Go to perdition, won't you!* Won't you quickly turn around and get yourself out of these halls?" (429–31). Now, however, Oedipus is intensely eager to hear (see 1170), and this scene enacts the Teiresias scene in reverse. Yet it parallels the first half of the Teiresias scene, too, in that, as he also did just before with Jocasta (1056–57), Oedipus brushes away someone's reluctance to speak.

Oedipus keeps narrowing the range of his questioning. Is he the Herdsman's own child? No. The child of a citizen of Thebes? The Herdsman balks, and Oedipus, unrelenting, perhaps even calm, forces him: "You are a dead man if I ask you this again" (1166). And so the Herdsman answers, but he still takes refuge in ambiguity, for his answer can mean either "a child of Laius" or "a child of someone in the household of Laius" (1167). Oedipus must then ask again, "A slave, or begotten by him, of his own race?" (1168).

The suspense does not let up, for Oedipus has a last, though faint, hope. To be proved to be a slave would be bitter and humiliating; it would deflate all the exuberance in the previous ode about being the child of a god. But the alternative is more bitter still, for Oedipus must remember Jocasta's account of the oracle given Laius, that he would "be killed by a child born from myself and him." This is indeed the "terrible point of speaking," as the Herdsman says, the moment he has dreaded all the years that he has lived with his secret, and Oedipus echoes his words: "Herdsman: I am at the uttermost terrible point of speaking. / Oedipus: And I of hearing, but hear I must" (1169–70). Oedipus's echo of the Herdsman's words verbally marks the strange kinship that has thus drawn together these two lives, the slave's and the king's.

"The woman inside would best tell how these things are" (1171-72), the Herdsman says, and the answer shifts perspective. Oedipus's thoughts at once go back to the mother. "She gave him to you?" "Yes, my lord." "For what purpose?" "To kill him." "The mother, poor woman?" "Yes, in fear of evil prophecies." "What?" "The tale was that he would kill his parents." And so the truth comes out, but with an unexpected show of feeling in Oedipus. In the previous scene he had cried out in surprise, almost pain, at the mention of his feet (1033) and asked whether that wound came "from the mother or the father" (1037). The scene before had showed a slight flutter of Oedipus's emotion toward family members when he reflected that his "father," Polybus, might have died out of longing for him (969-70). And at the end we shall see his deep concern for his children. Now, learning the truth, he thinks about the mother, perhaps in pity, perhaps in horror, anger, or revulsion, perhaps all the above, for his phrase in line 1175, "the mother, poor woman," can imply all of these feelings; and the word for "mother" here is not *mêtêr*, but *tekousa*, literally "she who gave birth."

It is worthwhile to pause over this phrase for a moment—actually only two words in Greek, *tlêmôn tekousa*—for it shows how difficult it is to translate Sophocles' density and richness of meaning. A translator must usually choose one meaning where the original implies two or more. Thus Richard C. Jebb translates the phrase as, "Her own child, the wretch?" David Grene renders it, "She was so hard—its mother?" Robert Fagles perhaps comes closest to the ambiguity with, "Her own child? How could she?" R. D. Dawe's paraphrase, in his commentary, catches both the particular nuance of *tekousa* and the ambiguity of *tlêmôn*: "After giving birth she must have been *unhappy to venture on* such a step."[6]

Having moved beyond his "terrible point of speaking," the Herdsman for the first time utters more than a line or two at a time. Pity was his motive for saving the baby, he says, as he explains how he gave the exposed infant to the Messenger (1177-81). There seems to be pity for the grown Oedipus too, as he tells him, "If you are the one whom this man says you are, then know that you have been born as an ill-starred man." Unknowingly, he echoes Jocasta's penultimate words to Oedipus, just before she ran inside the palace: "Ill-starred man, may you never know who you are" (1068).

Like Teiresias, the Herdsman knew a secret and was forced to tell it, but this simple, fearful man is at the opposite remove from the haughty, powerful prophet. Ironically, the deep truths that Teiresias pronounced were ignored, while this slave's little piece of truth brings Oedipus's whole world crashing down around him. Whereas Teiresias spoke his revelation in the pride and anger of an offended prophet, the Herdsman, simple as he is, speaks with pity. The Herdsman had spoken only of the one oracle that he knew about, namely that the child he saved would kill its parents (1176). Oedipus, now knowing all three oracles and having lived with the horror of his own oracle since adolescence, cries out in horror that "everything now has come out clearly" (1182). At this moment of awful clarity, as illusion turns into truth, vision turns into blindness. Calling on the light that he would see for the last time, he rushes into the palace with a string of short words, untranslatable in their sound and syntax, that conveys the interwoven curses of parricide and incest.

FOURTH STASIMON (FIFTH CHORAL ODE)

The ode that follows (1186–1222) releases the almost unbearable tension of Oedipus's discovery. Like many of the odes, it also serves to mark the passage of time—here the time during which Oedipus has entered the palace for his last great act. In contrast to the previous ode of hope and joyful anticipation that Oedipus will prove to be the son of a god, this fifth choral ode reflects on his fall from honor to utter misery and places his tragedy in the wider context of the uncertainty of all human happiness: "O generations of men, how I count you as equal to nothing while you live" (1186–88). This cry takes up the theme of counting when all of Oedipus's calculations have failed miserably. In contrast to the ageless laws of the gods spoken of in the second stasimon (863ff), mortal life appears in its fullest subjection to time, change, and the terrible entanglements of its begetting. In the previous scene, Oedipus exulted in the news of Polybus's death because it made the oracles "worth nothing" (971–72). Now his own birth has made him the chief example of the nothingness of all mankind.

The ode virtually passes in review all of Oedipus's great achievements, now that they have come to nothing: his conquest of the Sphinx, his protection of the city as its "tower," his great honor as ruler of Thebes (1198–1204). The "happiness" and "good fortune" on which the Messenger had congratulated his house (929) are now empty (1198). "Famous Oedipus," the chorus says, and the phrase ironically echoes his own confident term for himself in the opening scene (see 1208 and 8). Born from the "furrows" that he plowed, he finds all the relationships of his time-bound mortality to be filled with horror (1211–16). Time itself, which Oedipus had in a sense mastered in answering the Sphinx's riddle, has now "found him out" in the terrible riddle of his own life, his "marriage that is no marriage" (1213–15).

The ode completes a pattern of images and motifs that have been building throughout the play and turns them from strength to weakness: counting, equality, harbor, agriculture, vision, silence. It is important for the rest of the play, however, that Oedipus's achievements are not wiped out. The chorus reflects on what Oedipus meant to them when he was strong: "To use straight speech, I breathed in relief thanks to you and closed my eyes in sleep" (1220–22).[7]

10

Resolution: Tragic Suffering, Heroic Endurance

EXODOS (CLOSING MOVEMENT)

After the great crisis of the recognition scene, the chorus's general-
izations restore an atmosphere of calm and solemn expectation.
Their concern also assures an attentive hearing for the Messenger,
who now enters. His long speech holds a succession of horrors: first
Jocasta's suicide, then Oedipus's frenzied entrance to her chamber
to find the body, and finally his self-blinding.

The Messenger's introduction, though perhaps a little tenden-
tious, raises two points important for Oedipus's appearance in the
final scenes: purification and the distinction between involuntary
and self-chosen suffering:

> I tell you neither the waters of the Danube
> nor the Nile can wash this palace clean.
> Such things it hides, it soon will bring to light—
> terrible things, and none done blindly now,
> all done with a will. The pains
> we inflict upon ourselves hurt most of all.
> (Fagles's translation, 1227–31)

Greek tragedies tend to luxuriate in such accounts of physical suffering, generally narrated and rarely shown onstage—a tendency

they passed on to the Roman tragedian Seneca and thence to Elizabethan dramatists like Shakespeare and Webster.

The Messenger's abrupt-seeming announcement of Jocasta's
death immediately after these lines contains a pathos and an
extraordinary mixture of conversational dialogue and poetic phras-
ing typical of Sophocles' style. What the Messenger says in line
1235 is literally, "The divine head of Jocasta is dead." This was
fairly common Greek poetic idiom, however stilted it sounds in
English, and it casts an aura of epic dignity, grandeur, and sorrow
around the queen's death. But this idiom had another (and only
one other) occurrence in the play—namely, at line 950, when Oedipus enters to hear the ostensibly good news of Polybus's death. "O
dearest head of my wife, Jocasta," he says at that moment, and this
is the only time in the play that Oedipus addresses Jocasta by
name and uses the superlative, "dearest." Thus that moment of joy
and deep love echoes ironically and pathetically in the Messenger's
stark words, which mark the reversal of all happiness in the house
of Oedipus.

In a play so much concerned with the revelation and recovery
of a deeply buried past, the climactic acts of both characters face
backward. Jocasta, whose last speech the Messenger quotes,
recalls Laius and the ill-starred begetting of their child (1246–51).
Oedipus reenacts symbolically both the incest and the parricide by
"striking into" the palace and "striking" his eyes (1252, 1270), using
the same verb that he used of "striking Laius" (807). His breaking
through the closed double doors of Jocasta's chamber symbolically
reenacts the incest, entering places that should have remained
closed to him, especially as the "double doors" recall the "double
bedding" and "double field" that describe the incest just before
(1249, 1257). The word used for the "sockets" of his eyes in his self-
blinding is the word used for the "joints" of his ankles in Jocasta's
account of the exposure (718). It has been suggested that the eyes
are a symbolic substitution for the male genitals, so that the self-
blinding is also a symbolic act of self-castration—and in many societies castration is the punishment for incest.[1]

The frenzied shouting of Oedipus that the Messenger reports is
the climax of the panic that rose in him when Jocasta first mentioned the triple roads. His emotional violence here contrasts with
her quiet suffering. Whereas she left the stage stifling her despair in

a last brief cry, Oedipus shouts. Whereas she withdrew to her chamber for a moment of bitter memory and reflection just before her suicide (1240–50), Oedipus rushes about the palace and asks for a sword, whether to kill himself or Jocasta, or both, we do not know (1252–55).

Like Eurydice, Creon's wife, in *Antigone*, Jocasta takes her suffering inside, to the hidden, private enclosures of the house. Oedipus, in the next scene, will cry out to be shown "to all the Thebans" (1288), making a public and civic display of his crime and his punishment. A woman's grief, like her life, must be hidden away from the public life of the city. Despite Jocasta's earlier adroitness in resolving the quarrel between Creon and Oedipus and in receiving the Messenger, her place, at the last crisis in her life, is in the interior space that defined a woman's identity in classical Athens.[2]

The narrated but unseen events are overwhelming in their specific details and sensory impressions: the sound of Oedipus's cries and the sight of the hanging woman inside her chamber, the golden pins, the dark red flow of blood on Oedipus's beard. But these surface details of human suffering and pathos also belong to a larger pattern of mysterious divine action suggested, for example, in the presence of some "divinity" (*daimon*), as the Messenger says, that showed Oedipus the way to Jocasta's chamber (1258–59). The wider implications of Oedipus's pollution are also evoked in the metaphor of "black storm and bloody hail" for the wounds to Oedipus's eyes and in the repeated agricultural images of "seeds" and "plowfields" (1246, 1257). These metaphors evoke the catastrophic disharmony between man and nature caused by the pollution in the royal house. They remind us specifically of Apollo's warning of a "storm of blood" upon the city if the pollution is not expelled (100–101) and also of the plague's effect of sterility in the fields (25–27, 171–73).

The Messenger's speech ends with the motifs of sight and spectacle as he prepares us for the entrance of Oedipus. The actor now wearing a mask that shows his bloodied eyes, Oedipus returns to the stage through the palace doors into which he had rushed in horror at the end of the previous scene. The chorus's song of horror here (1296–1306) parallels the bitter ode on the nothingness of human life at the end of the previous scene (1186ff), but now general reflections on all of human life give way to an intense emotional cry in direct engagement with Oedipus and his pitiable appearance. It is a dreadful sight, they say, and it makes them "shudder" (1306). And now as well, Oedipus, for the first time in the play, joins the chorus in a lyrical exchange, a kind of duet, that begins with his outcries of pain and suffering. Hitherto he has spoken only in the dialogue or recitative meter of the iambic trimeter. By joining the chorus in the song meters, he expresses both a new level of emotion, in contrast to his previous control, and a new bond of sympathy and humanity, in contrast to his previous commanding distance.

If the Messenger's speech contains the climax of the action, the appearance of Oedipus immediately after is the climax of the drama as a visual spectacle. Instead of the proud king of the prologue, we see the anguished, blinded sufferer. Instead of confident speech and clear reasoning, we hear a series of monosyllabic cries and scarcely coherent exclamations:

> Where am I going? where on earth?
> where does all this agony hurl me?
> where's my voice?—
> winging, swept away on a dark tide—
> O dark power of the god, what a leap you made!
> (Fagles's translation [slightly modified], 1309–11)

Like Teiresias, Oedipus now needs a guide (1292–93), but with his weakness he also takes on something of Teiresias's vision of truth. Sophocles has frequently played on "Oedipus" as meaning "know where" (*oida pou,* "I know where").[3] The man who, as Teiresias said, did not know where he was in suffering or in his place among his closest kin (367, 413–15) now, in his physical blindness, when he literally does not know where, is shedding the figurative blindness of illusion and moving toward a clearer vision of his life.

The maxim of the oracular god Apollo at Delphi was "Know thyself," and this Oedipus has begun to do. This phrase, however, means not just to know one's idiosyncratic individual personality, in the sense in which a contemporary North American or European would speak of "finding yourself" or "expressing yourself." Rather, it refers to grasping the nature of mortal life and, in particular, the limitations that surround human life: the accidents of birth and unpredictable suffering or illness. In this sense Oedipus, as the previous ode suggested (1193–96), has begun to know himself as a mortal being, the example par excellence of human suffering and the precariousness of human fortunes. It is in this light that we can now understand the Priest's address to Oedipus in the opening scene as "first of men in the circumstances of life and in the meetings with divinities" (33–34). Oedipus now considers himself, as he says a little later, "of mortals the most hateful to the gods" (1345–46). Echoing the chorus, he calls himself "unfortunate" (1303, 1308), using the epithet that Jocasta had given him as her "last address" (1071). Oedipus has, in a sense, discovered his true name and his true mortal identity.

Whatever the events in his past that lay beyond his control, Oedipus has pushed through the errors and lies surrounding his life to reach this moment of dreadful clarity. Having recognized that his life hitherto has been founded on a horrible illusion, he makes the decision, based on full knowledge, to change its course radically. He insists on the distinction between the suffering that came from Apollo and his own self-chosen and self-inflicted punishment:

> Apollo, friends, Apollo—
> he ordained my agonies—these, my pains on pains!
> But the hand that struck my eyes was mine,
> mine alone—no one else—
> I did it all myself!
> What good were eyes to me?
> Nothing I could see could bring me joy.
> (Fagles's translation, 1328–35)[4]

Choice is important, and it marks Oedipus's strength, decisiveness, and moral clarity even in the midst of his sufferings.

When he returns from lyrical meter to iambic trimeter and so speaks more calmly, Oedipus makes a sustained, reasoned defense for blinding himself. What pleasure could he take in looking on his parents in the underworld or on his incestuously begotten children in this world (1369–90)? He might have merely killed himself, as Jocasta did. The chorus's questions, in fact, may be a tactful query as to why he did not simply commit suicide. Sophocles made Oedipus's endurance of the pain of his life even more dramatically effective by hinting at the possibility of suicide, both in his exit lines right after his discovery ("O light, may I look on you now for the last time" [1183]) and in his demand for a sword after he rushes into the palace (1255).[5]

Although Oedipus realizes that Apollo, not chance, has "leaped upon" him to cause his sufferings (compare 1311 with 263 and 469), he does not blame the god. He merely accepts divine will as the remote and mysterious source of the tragic pattern that life held for him. He knows, factually, that he has touched the deepest suffering possible for a human being (1365–66). He recognizes the cruel irony that the man who "saved" him from death in infancy has in fact been the source of disaster rather than comfort, and he curses his rescuer (1349–55). But, having survived, he now has the understanding to see his life as a whole and the strength to bear its terrible suffering.

THE HERO IN HIS SUFFERING

The last 200 lines, after the emergence of the blinded Oedipus from the palace, are an indispensable part of Sophocles' interpretation of the myth of Oedipus and need to be studied carefully. They express Sophocles' view of the tragic heroism of this great sufferer. Three aspects of Oedipus's situation are especially important.

First, Oedipus has decided to survive his horrifying discovery, to punish himself with blindness rather than death. In this he is the model for the heroic endurance of Euripides' Heracles in *Heracles Mad*, who makes the conscious decision to "resist misfortunes" and "endure life" after the madness in which he killed his wife and children (1347–51). Sophocles does not intellectualize the issue of suicide as Euripides does, however. When we see Oedipus returning, blinded to the stage, we know that he has passed through this dark moment and survived the worst that life can hold.[6]

Second, although Oedipus wants to be led away and expelled from Thebes as his curse requires, he is not alone. The chorus does not abandon him. Though they find his presence hideous, they do not turn away. They are full of pity, and he addresses them as "dear friends" for the first time in the play (*philoi*, 1321, 1329, 1339). He is moved and grateful to find them so concerned: "My friends, you still attend me, steadfast, for still you have the endurance to care for me in my blindness. O woe, O woe. Yet you are not hidden from me. In darkness though I am, I yet recognize your voice; I know it clearly" (1321-25).[7] Despite Oedipus's momentary wish to cut off all his channels of perception of the outside world (1386ff), he does not break his bond of closeness with his Theban citizens, now his "friends," nor does he hide himself away in shame and debasement.[8] Earlier he had asked to be "shown to all the Thebans" as the criminal that he is (1287ff), an act of moral courage worthy of a great ruler. Even in his despair he shows himself to be a king. It is tempting to draw a comparison with King Lear's equally tragic, though perhaps more pathetic, "Ay, every inch a king" (King Lear, 4.6.106).

Third, weak as he is, Oedipus has an inner strength, and this becomes surer and clearer as the scene goes on. The chorus says compassionately, "It is no wonder that amid such sufferings you have a double grief and endure double woes" (1319-20). Oedipus will soon take up their word "endure" as he himself comes to reflect on his growing strength (1415).

These three qualities of Oedipus—his ability to survive the torment both from the gods and from his own self-punishing remorse, his continuing bonds with his citizens and his family, and his inner strength in the midst of physical weakness—are not a program or a moralizing "message," nor do they appear in a simple linear progression. Rather, Sophocles shows us, in concrete emotional terms, a human being with deep resources of spirit who is afflicted with an overwhelming disaster of unpredictable, irrational suffering, but who is not totally annihilated by it. His dialogue with the chorus in lyrical meter (1307-66), as we have noted, expresses this new intensity of feeling.

Even after this lyrical passage, however, Oedipus continues to swing between bitterness and acceptance, despair and courage, especially in his two long speeches in lines 1369-1415 and 1446-75. We watch him groping his way toward what and who he now is. When the chorus, meaning well, agrees that he would have been better off dead, he snaps back, "Do not try to teach or counsel me that what I did was not done for the best" (1369-70). He still has the afterglow of the strength in his terrible decision, and although he values the chorus's concern for him, he also feels a

140

fierce justice in accepting the punishments that he had called down upon the killer when he was king. He has gone beyond where other men go and has little patience with banal condolences.

Oedipus is still struggling to come to terms with his new identity, and part of his struggle is a search for self-understanding through reviewing his life. He names the crucial places of his past—Cithaeron, Corinth, the triple road—and seems to impute a demonic quality to these places (1391ff). He personifies the triple road as a gigantic beast that drinks his and Laius's blood (1399–1401), and he rails bitterly against Cithaeron as the place destined by his parents to be his tomb, the place that buried the normal human existence from which he was cast out (1449–54).

Polybus and Corinth "nurtured" him, he says, as "something handsome with evils festering beneath the sore" (1394–96). He sees his life in a new way, as a delusive surface that has now been stripped away, but he also takes up the play's pervasive imagery of disease. Oedipus's very body is now revealed as the city's hidden disease. His word *nurtured* here also suggests that he is finally obeying Apollo's command, "Drive out the land's pollution as being nurtured in this earth" (96–97).

It is among the paradoxical reversals of illusion and reality, vision and blindness, that Oedipus, by bringing surface and depth together, is becoming more whole. The last statement of his long speech is remarkably calm: "It's all right. Touch the man of grief. / Do. Don't be afraid. My troubles are mine / and I am the only man alive who can sustain them" (Fagles's translation, 1413–15). In his growing strength Oedipus begins to act as the ritual scapegoat, the *pharmakos*, the figure who is ritually laden with all the evils and impurities of the community and then expelled to purify it.[9] Thus the Thebans need not fear pollution from his touch any longer. Oedipus has separated himself from the monstrous, polluted self that had been hidden within him for so long.

Creon's entrance at this point is brilliantly timed. Officially, he has replaced Oedipus as the king whose sacred function it is to assure harmonious relations between the human world and the forces of nature on which the city's life depends (1418). And yet that sacred office still essentially resides in Oedipus. Oedipus reiterates to Creon what he had asked of the chorus, namely that he be cast out of the land or killed, thereby fulfilling his own curse and what he took to be Apollo's command (1410-12, 1436-37).

Where Oedipus is passionate and eager for the expulsion to take place with all possible speed (1436), Creon is cautious and unsure. He hesitates to act on his own authority, and he once more sends to Delphi to inquire of Apollo (1438-43). The short exchange brings the play back to the opening situation, but with Creon now in the role of king, sending an emissary to Delphi to ask what to do about the pollution. The contrast between the two men sets into relief the energy, efficiency, and confidence that brought Oedipus his success—and his ruin.

Oedipus continues to fight down waves of bitterness and despair. Though he asks to be thrown forth to dwell on the wild Cithaeron that his parents destined for his death (1449-54), he abruptly turns away from thoughts of dying: "And yet I know this much: no disease or anything else would have destroyed me, for I would not have been saved from dying except for something terrible. Let my life's portion go wherever it will go" (1455-58). It is a remarkable and important statement, a broad vision of a whole life, from earliest childhood to the present. His was a life dominated by rejection, suffering, and death from the very first, and with no clear reason for the suffering. And yet Oedipus affirms the inner strength equal to the suffering. In the scene just before, speaking to the chorus of Theban elders, Oedipus called for his death or expulsion as the land's pollution but then saw himself as touchable again, since "no one of mortals except myself can bear my woes" (1414-15). Now, speaking to Creon, he repeats and exceeds that spirit of endurance and accepts the tragic shape or "portion" of his life as a whole.

Sophocles has chosen this moment of courage for another surprise. Addressing Creon by name for the first time in the scene (1459), Oedipus asks him to look after his children—not the boys, who are already "men," but his "wretched, piteous two daughters," Antigone and Ismene, who always shared his table (1460-65). The detail illustrates Oedipus's capacity for affection and sense of his responsibility for his family as well as for his city. He has also moved beyond self-pity. Here he begins to free himself from the past's dark burden and to think of the future; he asks for the burial of Jocasta and for the care of his children. For the first time we see

Oedipus speaking as a father, not to his city but to his own offspring.

When Oedipus asks Creon not to make his daughters "equal to his own sufferings" (1507), we can see Sophocles reshaping the Aeschylean treatment of the legend. Instead of cursing his sons, Oedipus invokes the responsibility of fatherhood and asks for Creon's help, "since you are left as the only father to these two girls" (1503–4). The chorus, shortly before, introduced Creon to Oedipus as "left as the only ruler of the land instead of you" (1418). Oedipus thus resigns to Creon his place as the father of his family, but in both cases he continues to be concerned for those whom his curse demands that he leave behind.

In a further surprise, the girls appear onstage, another bold stroke on Sophocles' part. Oedipus, who, as he said, had no use for vision, is eager for touch. He thanks Creon for his pity and welcomes them into his arms (1480ff). In the first line of the play Oedipus, as king, had addressed his citizens as "children." He now addresses his actual children with the same word (1480), but with the horrible resonances of the pollutions of incest and parricide, for "children" is here coupled with "sisters" in the next line (1481).

In contrast to the concealment of the incestuous relation in the past and his horror when it came to light, Oedipus now faces his crime squarely, in grimly familiar agricultural imagery. Born where the "sowing" in the "double field" was wrongly fertile, his daughters will be left unmarried, as "barren soil" (1497–1502). Acknowledging his helplessness, Oedipus again asks for pity (1507), calls Creon "noble"—a far cry from his insults of their last meeting—and asks for the touch of his hand (1510). Throughout the scene it is important for Oedipus to establish the human contact of touch with those close to him, despite the terrible pollution that he knows he bears (see 1413, 1469, 1481ff).

Creon's matter-of-fact authority checks the outpouring of emotion. He calls for an end of weeping and separates Oedipus from his daughters, to which Oedipus reluctantly agrees. Despite the reversal of roles, however, something fundamental in the two men remains unchanged. When Creon, close to the end, tells Oedipus, "I am not accustomed to speak vainly about what I do not understand" (1520), he is repeating almost verbatim what he had said about Teiresias when Oedipus had accused him of conspiring with the prophet (569). And he still admonishes Oedipus about his exercise of power (1522–23). With these lines, marking the formal end of that role as King of Thebes with which he began, Oedipus is slowly led back into the palace while Creon's attendants lead his daughters offstage.

Sophocles may have ended his play here. The extant manuscripts have seven additional verses, in which the chorus addresses the citizens of Thebes and moralizes on Oedipus's fall and the uncertainty of human fortunes (1524–30). Scholars are divided as to whether Sophocles himself wrote these lines; many hold that they were added later, for use by acting companies. Aside from a number of grammatical problems, it is suspicious that they closely resemble the ending of Euripides' *Phoenician Women*, written some 20 years after *Oedipus Tyrannus*. The banal moralizing achieves closure, to be sure, but might not Sophocles have wanted the more austere ending? Such would be the effect of closing with Creon's words in lines 1522–23, "Do not wish to exercise power in everything, for even those things over which you were powerful did not follow along with you in life."

THE CLOSING SCENE

It is hard for a modern audience to gauge the tone of the final scene. Modern taste may balk at the presence of the young girls beside a bloodstained father who speaks frankly of their incestuous birth. But the ancient audience was far less squeamish about children's feelings. In Euripides' *Alcestis* and *Suppliant Women* small children are present at their mother's death and lament over her body.

The visual spectacle reinforces the range and power of emotions. There are contrasts in pollution and loving touch, isolation and the bonds of family, Oedipus's helplessness and his growing inner clarity, his dependence and his continuing sense of authority. In a play whose chief effect is reversal, the closing scene forms the antithesis to the opening. Now Creon is in command, and Oedipus is the subordinate. Instead of being the receiver of supplication, Oedipus is the suppliant and asks for pity. Oedipus began as a

proud king, "called famous by all," as he says of himself in the first
scene (8), surrounded by a throng of admiring, respectful subjects;
he is now set apart from all men as the disease of the city.

Modern directors are sometimes tempted to make the last
scene turbulent and gory, emphasizing the contrast between the
bloodstained king/criminal and the still-innocent young daughters.[10] But what is perhaps most striking about the ending is its
calm and its emphasis on pity and the power of human ties in the
midst of all the horror. One must not sentimentalize. There is still
deep bitterness in Oedipus, still an imperious will. But he also has
the simplicity of his greatness. He can ask for pity and try to shelter
those he loves from the hard life that he knows awaits them.
Despite his isolation and the sufferings of his house and his city, he
helps reknit the bonds of family and society. Although he is no
longer king, his appeals to the elders and to Creon help the curse-
driven city to regain its health as a human community.

In the last movement Sophocles scales the action down from
the political and natural realms to the personal ties within the family. Even Creon, for all his hesitation, shows pity and understanding. Oedipus would give his daughters fatherly advice and hope for
a better life than his, and seeks to enlist Creon as a kind of surrogate father (1503ff). But he cannot cease being Oedipus the King;
and Creon, the lesser man, senses his lingering will to power and
so admonishes Oedipus to take a more submissive attitude.

The actual fate of Oedipus is left suspended. We do not know
whether he will be exiled or will remain in Thebes. Both stories
were current in the fifth century. In one sense it does not matter,
for the inner drama of Oedipus is completed when he brings his
doomed infancy on Cithaeron together with his present life in
Thebes and rejects the death that the former moment held.

The play shows the birth of a type of hero new to Sophoclean
drama: a figure who is neither crushed by his suffering, as Creon is
at the end of *Antigone*, nor an egotist of violent pride who would
rather die than live with his shame, like Ajax. In the (probable)
chronological order of the extant plays, Oedipus is the first protagonist who does not commit suicide. The closest analogy, as was
suggested earlier, is the Heracles of Euripides' *Heracles Mad*, written perhaps a few years after *Oedipus Tyrannus* and possibly influenced by it. Euripides' hero, sustained by the companionship of

Theseus, can survive the horror of having murdered his family in a fit of madness. But Heracles is the son of Zeus and openly pursued by hostile gods; Oedipus is purely human, and the role of the gods is kept remote.

Oedipus's concern for his children at the end completes another pattern in his life. He cannot, of course, cancel out the incest, but he can transform its monstrosity into something humanly bearable. When his father had struck him at the cross-roads, Oedipus made him "pay back no equal share" in turning the blow back fatally upon the attacker (810). Now he asks Creon not to make his daughters "equal to my evil sufferings" (1506). He does not perpetuate in his own life his father's aggression against his child. Reading backwards from this final scene, one perhaps recalls Oedipus's sudden bursts of anxious curiosity about whether his mother or his father exposed him for death on the mountain (1037, 1173–76). In regarding his daughters with compassion rather than with abhorrence, violence, or rejection, and in trying to provide for their future, he has drastically reversed the treatment that he received from Laius and Jocasta.

The ending, while full of the horror of great suffering, is not cast in a mood of hopelessness or despair. Oedipus's fear for himself made him rather callous about his supposed father's death (a gentler replay of his killing of his real father, Laius), but after his passage through the anguish of discovery and self-punishment he has pity for his daughters' future and concern for the decent burial of Jocasta. He has become the paradigm not only of the fragile, uncertain condition of mortality, but also of the courage and spiritual strength of humanity. With his self-inflicted punishment for his past, and by assuming responsibility for those ties of blood and family in the present, Oedipus overcomes in himself the animal brutishness of incest and parricide.

After his frenzied rush into the palace at the moment of discovery, Oedipus's calm at the end is neither Stoic resignation nor Christian remorse. He sees himself as still "hated by the gods" (1519) but does not rant against them or immerse himself in guilt. He belongs to a culture in which the mere fact of having performed the acts of parricide and incest leaves an indelible stain or pollution, regardless of the motivations or intentions. He accepts the objective fact of being horribly polluted, and he can live with the inner torment of knowing these crimes. This continuing torment is expressed in his decision to live the rest of his life in blindness. In his long speeches to the chorus and to Creon he struggles with accepting his life's pattern, his "portion," in the fearful form that it has come to have (see 1413–15, 1455–58).

"Most hateful to the gods," Oedipus calls himself in what is nearly his final utterance onstage (1519). In the last scene Creon is sending to Delphi to ask a question of one of these gods, just as Oedipus did in the first scene. Sophocles does not tell us what anwer Apollo will give to Creon. By concluding the play in this manner, Sophocles is not just showing us Creon's prudence or marking a circularity of structure; he is leaving us with a question. Oedipus has, in a sense, already received his answer in the events that followed his own inquiry, but it is an answer that only leads us to ask deeper questions about the gods and their role in human life.

Oedipus's tragic success in discovering himself as Laius's killer and thus as the source of the pollution presumably ends the plague of Thebes. Yet the silence about the plague at the end of the play also sets off the new course Oedipus's life has taken. He is no longer merely a hero of external victories and rewards. Along with his change of focus comes his shift from weeping over the city's woes in the first scene to his weeping over the sufferings within his family at the play's end (66 and 1486). He has become a hero of inner vision and personal suffering. Indeed, it is precisely by showing Oedipus's life against its earlier success and power that Sophocles defines it as tragic and thus creates the form of the "tragic hero" in Western literature: a figure whose force of personality and integrity set him (or her) apart for a special destiny and enable him to confront that destiny with clarity and courage after a painfully won struggle for self-knowledge.[11]

11

Inner Vision and
Theatrical Spectacle

SEEN AND UNSEEN

The theatrical spectacle of *Oedipus Tyrannus* works as much by what is not said and not shown as by the spoken and visible elements of the performance. Certain things are more powerful for being left unsaid and unseen. Such is the case with the events in the two long narratives, one by Oedipus and one by the Messenger. The first describes the death of the father, Laius, at the blow of the son's *skeptron*, the staff or scepter that Oedipus carries; the second describes the death of the mother, Jocasta, and the self-blinding of the son. Both scenes are left hidden, without visual enactment, so that they may be played out all the more effectively in the interior theater of our imaginations. In this way Sophocles gives us a glimpse of what psychoanalytic critics have called the "other scene," the imaginary place where the repressed fears and wishes of the unconscious are played out.[1]

The two narratives of crucial past events in *Oedipus Tyrannus* are complementary scenes of horrible violence involving the death of parents. In their presentation of a son's aggression against a father and the death of a mother, they resemble Freud's primal scenes: traumatic experiences that disturb emotional development because they stir up deep fears or anxieties about one's basic identity or view of the self—like a young child's witnessing of parental

148

intercourse. Both scenes in the play are enacted in the nonvisual medium of a buried memory.

The second narrative, the tale of Jocasta's death, begins with the Messenger's qualification, "Of what was done the most painful things are absent, for vision was not present" (1238–39). The "absence" of the pain is symmetrical with the nonpresence of the "vision." But, the Messenger goes on, he will tell "the suffering of that unhappy woman" in so far as his memory permits (1239). The collocation of presence and absence in his first line is appropriate to the indirect mode of narration used here (as opposed to the direct mode of dramatic enactment onstage) and to the necessarily partial recovery of lost events through memory.

Sophocles takes pains to show us how we *know* what we *see* in this crucial scene. The Messenger's memory leads us verbally into the interior chamber of Jocasta's marriage bed (1241–42). He tells how Jocasta "closes the doors" with violence behind her "when she went inside" (1244). The narrative relies on the medium of sound to reveal what occurred in the chamber. Those left *outside* heard a voice from *within*. But the account also includes something more than the voice—namely, memory (the Greek word *mnema* here [1246] includes both "memory" and "mention"). This "remembering" by Jocasta is deeper and more painful than the Messenger's "memory" eight lines before, and it takes us into the remoter past: "When she went *inside* the doors, she dashed them closed *inside* and calls on Laius now *long since* a corpse, having *memory* [making mention] of the sowing [seeds] of *long ago*, by which he himself died, but left behind the mother of a child for ill-starred childmaking with his own" (1244–48; my italics).[2] The repetition "Laius *long since* a corpse" and the "sowing of *long ago*," combined with the emphasis on memory (1239, 1246), reinforces the movement back to the past. Jocasta brings to her mind (and ours) the night when Laius made her pregnant with Oedipus ("the sowing of long ago"). Her reported gesture of closing the doors behind her as she calls up this memory from her first marriage prepares the way for the symbolic reenactment of her second, incestuous marriage in the ensuing narrative, with the son now replacing the father.[3] She, recalling her union with Laius, her last "memory" in life, closes the gates. Oedipus bursts into the palace and asks for a sword, searching for Jocasta (1252ff).

The following action of the narrative recalls the crimes of Oedipus's past as well. The weapon that he seeks now, however, is one of penetration (1255), different from the staff/scepter, the weapon he used to club Laius at the crossroads. He then forcibly "drives into the double gates," "pushes inward the hollow bolts," and "falls into the chamber" (1261–62). He thus forces his way into the mother's closed, "hollow" (1262), interior space, the private chamber that she had barred behind her as she remembered those "seeds" of Laius in the past (1246).

Here, in this place of terror, the events are envisioned through memory rather than in the immediacy of present event: "There was no vision," said the Messenger, "but yet, as far as lies in my *memory*, you will learn her sufferings" (1238–39). The emphasis on memory is striking when one considers how much memory has distorted the recollection of the past in the play. Jocasta, Oedipus, the Herdsman have all been shown to have highly selective memories (1057, 1131; see also 870–71). Memory is here correlative with vision, a kind of nonvisual seeing.

The Messenger's tale not only presents the visual contents of memory but is also an emblematic account of memory's inner vision, for it consists in gradual penetration into increasingly interior and hidden spaces (1239–96). The memory of the Messenger conducts us inside the gates of the palace, where Oedipus rushes around in wild despair. Then it shows us the interior space of Jocasta's marriage chamber, the scene of her suicide and Oedipus's self-blinding. These most important events are forbidden to open vision and are accessible only in fragments, by significant absence rather than through the full presence of the actors or the enacted events. By calling attention to the fact that he is withholding the visual appearance of his chief protagonists in favor of a purely verbal narration, the poet also reveals his own consciousness of the theatrical spectacle as a special form of narrative, mediating between external and interior vision, between visible, physical acts and the emotional world they reveal.

Oedipus's very act of forcible entry creates another blockage of vision and thus deprives the Messenger of certain, visual knowledge of the details. "How after this she perished," the Messenger goes on, "I know no further, for Oedipus, shouting, broke his way in, and by his act it was no longer possible to behold, as in a spectacle, her woe. But rather we turned our gaze toward him as he roamed around" (1251–54). Vision again becomes blurred in the vagueness of the Messenger's report that some unnamed divinity (*daimon*) "showed" Oedipus the way (1258), "not any one of us men who were present nearby" (1259). The "men" are concrete forms, "nearby," visible, and familiar; the unknown *daimon* (the vaguest possible term for a god or supernatural agent) is invisible, mysterious, undefined.

Sophocles makes our vision of the narrated events deliberately elusive. Vision was blocked first by the closing of doors (1241ff), then by the violent acts and shouts of Oedipus in the palace (1252–53), and finally by his presence over the body of Jocasta (1264ff). After Oedipus has broken down the doors we onlookers are allowed to "see into" the firmly shut chamber (1263). The further penetration of the eye inward, into increasingly inward and hidden space, culminates in Oedipus's "seeing" of Jocasta (1265), the goal and result of his forced entry into the locked, forbidden place. From that point, vision is again permitted, although still through the indirect mode of third-person narration. It is now a vision characterized by that quality of the "terrible" that broods over the play from the beginning and finally becomes visible in the spectacle of "things terrible to look upon" (1267; see also 1297, 1306, 1312).

The last object of sight, "the things terrible to look upon," is the physical act of putting an end to vision: Oedipus's tearing the pins from Jocasta's robes and striking his eyes. It is reported not as the result of an active verb of seeing, as in the lines immediately preceding—"we saw within," "he sees her" (1263 and 1265)—but in an impersonal way: "From that point there were things terrible to see." It is as if this seeing is already formed into a tableau, a final memorable sight, fixed self-consciously as the result of a narrative of unforgettable power but not in fact shown on the stage. When the pervasive terror reaches it climax, "no spectacle is present" (1238). Such are the terrible things that the unstaged spectacle has finally to show.

The horror of the sight is now matched by the horror of the sound. This too comes to us indirectly, by report. Jocasta's "call" to the dead Laius (1245) and her "lament" over her marriage bed (1249) fade into the silence of her still-mysterious death ("how after this she perished I do not know" [1251]). The sounds we now hear come from Oedipus: he "shouts" (1252) as he breaks his way into the palace, "cries terrible things" as he forces his way into Jocasta's chamber (1260), "roars terribly" at what he sees there (1265), and "shouts" again as he strikes his eyes (1271). The crescendo of horror reached in this last cry recapitulates the horror in the scene as whole, for it repeats the "terrible shouting" as he forced the doors open 10 lines before (1260). The accompanying action, the "striking" of his eyes (*epaisen*, 1270), also repeats his first entry into the palace, when he "struck" his way inside (*eisepaisen*, 1252).

Oedipus's last shout is itself closely linked to vision, for he cries that "his eyes will never see the things that he has suffered or the things that he has done" (1271-72). The same verbs of shouting then recur fewer than 20 lines later, when the Messenger describes how Oedipus, still offstage, "shouts out to open the enclosing gates" (1287-88). These are no longer the doors of private, interior chambers but the public gates of the palace that will reveal to all the Thebans the fearful spectacle that he has become.

The anticipation of Oedipus's entrance heightens the tension between what is described verbally through narration and what is shown visually as theatrical spectacle. The doors of the palace open, and the Messenger describes this action: "These enclosures of the gates are opening" (1294-95). But he is also echoing, now in his own words, the words of Oedipus that he had just quoted, "Open the enclosures and show to all the Thebans" (1287-88).[4] "Soon you will see a spectacle," the Messenger continues to the chorus, "such that even the one who loathes it will feel pity" (1295-96). It is as if the playwright/director were telling his audience how he is utilizing the visual effects of his medium. The chorus, like the audience that now beholds the palace doors opening, gives voice to the proper theatrical response, again in visual terms: "O suffering terrible for men to *look upon*" (1297; my italics). The obverse of the present spectacle—the blinded king with his bloodied eyes—is the unseen spectacle of the closed interior chamber where Jocasta died: "It was not possible to behold as in a spectacle her [Jocasta's] suffering" (1258).

The relation between text and action stresses the parallelism and the contrast between verbally describing the unseen events behind the palace and bedchamber doors and theatrically showing

Oedipus as a spectacle onstage. He now emerges through the palace doors as the center of all attention and the object of pitiable *sight* for all. "O suffering terrible for men to look upon" is the immediate response of the chorus (1297). Sophocles thus calls attention to the double mode of narration going on before us, the visual enactment and the verbal telling. The Messenger's tale, in which "there is no vision present" (1238), parallels the spectacle on the stage and before our eyes: it too is a way of "opening doors" to the hidden events that arouse our terror and our pity.

DRAMA AND THE INTERIOR VISION

This withholding of vision and partial access to vision in a story that culminates in the destruction of eyes are among the means by which Sophocles stamps the narration with its characteristic feature, a reluctance to emerge into the light, a tale of horror that wants to remain hidden in the darkness of the unseen. Teiresias's blind seeing, reluctant speech, and uncomprehended utterances in the meeting with Oedipus early in the play formed the first explicit model onstage for a story that refused to be told and a knowledge that refused to be known. Now, at the most intense point of the action, during the Messenger's narration, the suppression of vision and speech moves to the center of the narrative. Not only does the refusal to see and to say everywhere pervade this telling, but it is also through this powerful "won't tell" that the story in fact gets itself told.

The climactic scene is recovered (as we have noted) only by a series of gradual movements backwards into the past and by a steady progression into a closed interior in the present. The discontinuous rhythm of exposure and concealment, vision and nonvision, closing off perception and removing blocking objects, is a symbolic condensation of Oedipus's past. The narrative that unfolds before us contains the climax of a tragic life and is simultaneously a microcosm of that pattern of events that gave such a life its tragic form.

When Oedipus has broken down the doors and does at last see Jocasta's body in her chamber, the first thing he does after "releasing" her from the noose is to "pull off the gold-beaten pins [*peronai*] from her garments, [the pins] with which she was dressed" (1268–69). This is the first of "the things terrible to see" (1267) to be described. *Peronai* are not merely decorative brooches, as the word is frequently translated, but the long pins that hold the robes together. Their removal could suggest the gesture of undressing the queen in her "marriage chamber" (1242) as she "lies there" (1267). If so, the gesture is a grotesque and horrible reenactment of the first night of their union. This is the act for which he "strikes the sockets of his eyes" in the next line, immediately cancelling out in himself the vision that his violation of her chamber has opened up to the audience. If the body of the king becomes that through which the invisible truth is made reality, the body of Jocasta points to something that remains inaccessible to vision and must remain hidden.

In an essay that has only recently become available to the English-speaking world, Vladimir Propp has analyzed numerous folk tales of the Oedipus type. Generally, he finds, the identity of the incestuous husband/son is discovered in the marriage bed by the presence of a scar or other mark, sometimes on the wedding night itself.[5] (Jean Cocteau brilliantly plays with this age-old motif of discovery on the wedding night in the bridal scene of his *Infernal Machine* [see Chapter 3].) Sophocles, however, withholds that recognition until it can bring only the tragic revelation of indelible pollution. But he retains the sexual component of the knowledge by implying the physical union in a series of symbolic equivalents: the penetration of the queen's closed chambers and the removal of the pins from the robes on her recumbent body.

There is a suggestive parallel to this scene in Sophocles' *Trachinian Women*. Deianeira, having discovered that what she thought was a love-charm is in fact a poison that is killing Heracles, goes to her bedchamber inside the house (923–26). After addressing her marriage bed for the last time, she stabs herself:

> She says nothing more, but with a violent sweep
> of her arm unfastens her gown where a pin
> of beaten gold lies above her breast. She had
> uncovered the whole side of her left arm.[6]

This unusually masculine form of death (women in Greek tragedy, like Jocasta or Phaedra, generally commit suicide by hanging) is not only part of the instability of male and female roles that runs throughout the play; it also marks a symbolic *Liebestod* (death-in-love) that takes the place of the union of husband and wife in the house. Both scenes make use of the sexual symbolism involved in the loosening of a woman's robe in her interior chamber, in close proximity to the conjugal bed. Horrible as the implications of such a scene are for Jocasta in *Oedipus Tyrannus*, they are none the less strongly present. Sophocles does not always show us things that are nice: we may recall Philoctetes' pus-soaked rags in *Philoctetes* or Ajax's corpse still blowing dark blood from the nostrils in *Ajax.*

This symbolic reenactment of incest in Oedipus and Jocasta's final union-in-death is part of the temporal enlargement and complication of the action that Sophocles exercises on the myth through the device of superimposing present acts on the remote past. Actions in the present both recall and reenact actions in the past, and the past seems always to be pulling the protagonists back, no matter how hard they try to escape it. This pull of the past contributes to the play's atmosphere of tragic necessity: something surrounding the lives of the chief characters that they cannot escape.

By lengthening the temporal perspective through the motif of discovering and remembering a long-forgotten past, Sophocles also calls attention to the representational power of drama, through which a single action unfolding onstage can contain, symbolically, the meaning of an entire lifetime. In the condensed temporal frame of Oedipus's life, the tragedian finds also a mirror image of his manipulation of time in the artistic construction of his play.

Greek tragedy has no word for "the self." As John Jones, arguing from Aristotle's *Poetics*, maintains, tragedy concentrates on exterior forms and events, on plot (*mythos*) as a concatenation of actions (*pragmata*).[7] Yet the sense of a self, of a complex inner life of motives, desires, and fears, is everywhere implicit. How does the tragedian make the inner life of the self visible? Where does it appear? Not onstage but in that action occurring behind the stage implied by the invisible text; something *there* but not representable, or representable only as a tension between the seen and the unseen. This interplay between interior and exterior space parallels the increasing awareness of the interior realm of the individual personality, and we see it also in Euripides' psychological exploration of motives in works like *Medea* and *Hippolytus*, and in Socrates' emphasis on knowledge and the soul. Greek drama has no general theory about what personality is, but, rather, it poses the self as problem. The Greeks raised with exceptional clarity the fundamental questions involved in representing "reality" in art.

In the conventions of Greek drama, the interior space of house or palace is not represented on the stage but is often implicit behind the action. The poet composed for a stage that shows only the outside, but that exterior face of the represented world has a depth of meaning derived in part from its hidden interior. That hidden inner scene corresponds both to the emotional life of the characters and, at some level, to the personal, imaginative vision of the poet, whose act of composition takes place before and apart from the public performance in the theater, where his words are given full realization.

The dramatist is a performance artist who manipulates real bodies in real space on the stage, but he is also a poet/writer who fashions myths into stories about passions, with the freedom of his plastic medium of words. Sophocles worked with the visible, public space of the open-air theater of Dionysus to reveal truths about hidden or invisible areas of existence that his poetry could call up in the imagination. Although the publicly enacted dimension of this art form was the most important to its original audience, who responded to it primarily as theater, its more private, psychological dimension remains rich with insights for the modern reader, who is more likely to approach these works as written texts.[8]

Oedipus Tyrannus is above all a great drama, but it also contains hints of the poet's awareness of the problem of representing reality, and especially the inner reality of the emotional life. This concern is particularly present in Sophocles' attention to what is shown and what is seen in the climactic scene of Oedipus's discovery of the buried truth, followed by his display of himself from the hitherto hidden interior of the palace. Revealing to an audience what is concealed behind doors and gates—the gates of the palace, of the mouth, or of the body—is not only a matter of practical dramaturgy. It is also the poet's reflection on the way that his art probes the dark side of life and the hidden depths of the soul, and on the way that our fascination with the spectacle makes us, like Oedipus, see what we would rather not see and know what we would prefer not to know.

Notes

1. Historical and Cultural Background

1. The term, in common use, is the subtitle of W. K. C. Guthrie's *A History of Greek Philosophy*, vol. 3 (Cambridge: Cambridge University Press, 1969). For the history and use of the term see Guthrie, page 48.

2. Victor Ehrenberg, in his *Sophocles and Pericles* (Oxford: Blackwell, 1954), has made the strongest case for viewing *Oedipus Tyrannus* as a conservative Sophocles' warning against Periclean rationalism.

3. Bernard M. W. Knox, *Oedipus at Thebes* (New Haven: Yale University Press, 1957), chap. 2, esp. pp. 64–106.

4. See Peter Euben, *The Tragedy of Political Theory* (Princeton: Princeton University Press, 1990), 99ff.

2. Why Read Oedipus Tyrannus?

1. Richmond Lattimore, *The Poetry of Greek Tragedy* (Baltimore: Johns Hopkins University Press, 1957), 99–100.

3. Reception and Influence

1. This information is given in the Argument prefixed to some of the medieval manuscripts of Sophocles' plays and is not elsewhere attested.

2. Suetonius, *Life of Julius Caesar*, chap. 56, and *Life of Nero*, chaps. 21 and 46.

3. Two of these illuminated manuscripts are illustrated in John Boswell, *The Kindness of Strangers: The Abandonment of Children in Western Europe from Late Antiquity to the Renaissance* (New York: Pantheon Books, 1988), plates 2 and 3, after p. 270. The tendency to make Oedipus's conflict with the Sphinx physical rather than intellectual runs throughout the history of the myth, from the fifth century B.C. on (see Chapter 5).

4. See R. R. Bolgar, *The Classical Heritage and its Beneficiaries* (Cambridge: Cambridge University Press, 1954), 504.

5. A variant of this view, with the figures reversed, is put forth (but as interpretation, not fiction) by Philip Vellacott, in *Sophocles and Oedipus*

(Ann Arbor: University of Michigan Press, 1971), 104ff. Oedipus, Vellacott argues, knows the truth all along and wants to lead Jocasta to acknowledging it.

6. André Gide, *Oedipus*, trans. John Russell, in *Oedipus: Myth and Dramatic Form*, ed. James L. Sanderson and Everett Zimmerman (Boston: Houghton Mifflin, 1968), 155.

7. Jean Cocteau, *The Infernal Machine*, trans. Carl Wildman, in *Oedipus: Myth and Dramatic Form*, 182.

8. Francis Fergusson, *The Idea of a Theater* (Garden City, N.Y.: Doubleday Anchor Books, 1955), 212. I have kept Fergusson's translation of Teiresias's remark here.

9. For a recent discussion of the relation between *Oedipus Tyrannus* and Pynchon's novel, see J. Peter Euben, *The Tragedy of Political Theory* (Princeton: Princeton University Press, 1990), 59–63, 281–308.

10. T. S. Eliot, *The Waste Land*, part 3, ll. 218ff.

11. For some of the African and Muslim versions see Colette Astier, *Le mythe d'Oedipe* (Paris: Armand Colin, 1974), 125–29, and Jacques Scherer, *Dramaturgies d'Oedipe* (Paris: Presses Universitaires de France, 1987), 176–79.

4. Performance, Theater, and Social Context

1. See Simon Goldhill, "The Great Dionysia and Civic Ideology," in *Nothing to Do with Dionysus?*, ed. John J. Winkler and F. Zeitlin (Princeton: Princeton University Press, 1990), 97–129, especially 98–106.

2. A few plays on contemporary subjects, however, were composed early in the fifth century, probably as a result of the stirring historical events of the Persian War. Aeschylus's *Persians* (472 B.C.) is the sole surviving example.

5. The Oedipus Myth and Its Interpretation

1. *Papyrus Lille*, 73 and 76 (1977). For the relevant text, translation, and interpretation see Charles Segal, "Archaic Choral Lyric," *Cambridge History of Classical Literature*, vol. 1, ed. P. Easterling and B. M. W. Knox (Cambridge: Cambridge University Press, 1985), 197–200.

2. Euripides also wrote a play based on this myth, *Chrysippus*, now lost. It was probably presented along with the *Phoenician Woman* in 409 B.C.

3. The fact that the only reference to the Fury in *Oedipus Tyrannus* comes from Teiresias (417–18) may be an indication that Sophocles substituted the prophet, who, after all, is still a human figure, for the supernatural and demonic power of the Fury.

13. Hegel's views are most easily accessible in Anne and Henry Paolucci, eds., *Hegel on Tragedy* (Garden City, N.Y.: Anchor Books, 1962), esp. 279–80, 325–26.

14. Friedrich Nietzsche, *The Birth of Tragedy* (1872), chap. 9, in *The Birth of Tragedy and the Genealogy of Morals*, trans. Francis Golffing (Garden City, N.Y.: Doubleday, 1956), 61.

15. Propp, "Oedipus in the Light of Folklore," 84–89.

16. For versions of this approach, with discussion of previous scholarship, see Edmunds and Dundes, *Oedipus: A Folklore Casebook*, 161–64; also Propp, "Oedipus in the Light of Folklore," 85.

17. See Propp, "Oedipus in the Light of Folklore," 76–121, 149. A useful brief survey of various interpretations of the myth may be found in Edmunds, *Oedipus: Ancient Legend*, 1–46; see also Martin P. Nilsson, *The Mycenaean Origin of Greek Mythology* (Berkeley and Los Angeles: University of California Press, 1932), 101–12.

18. Sigmund Freud, *The Interpretation of Dreams*, 3d ed., trans./ed. James Strachey (New York: Basic Books, 1955), 296; hereafter cited in text.

19. Sigmund Freud, "Dostoevsky and Parricide," in *The Standard Edition of the Complete Psychological Works of Sigmund Freud*, ed. James Strachey (London: Hogarth Press, 1961), vol. 21, 188. The essay dates from

20. Sigmund Freud, *A General Introduction to Psychoanalysis*, trans. Riviere (New York: Liverwright, 1935), 291.

. Freud, "Dostoevsky and Parricide," 188.

Freud, *A General Introduction to Psychoanalysis*, 291.

The refocusing of the work of the unconscious on the processes of is implicit in Freud (see his famous essays "The Antithetical Sense Words" and "Negation" and his analysis of language practiced in *ology of Everyday Life* and *Jokes in their Relation to the Unconscious* it is especially developed in the work of Jacques Lacan (see his *ection*, trans. A. Sheridan [New York: Norton, 1977] and *Speech ge in Psychoanalysis*, trans. A. Wilden [Baltimore: Johns Hopkins ty Press, 1968].)

Paul Ricoeur, *Freud and Philosophy*, trans. D. Savage (New niversity Press, 1970), 519.

e Lévi-Strauss, "The Structural Study of Myth," in *Structural ns. C. Jacobson and B. C. Schoepf (Garden City, N.Y.: Dou 02–28, esp. 210–13.

robing critique of Lévi-Strauss's interpretation within the l of the myth, see Terence S. Turner, "Narrative Structure A Critique and Reformulation of Structuralist Concepts of d Poetics," *Arethusa* 10 (1977): 103–63.

4. For the exposure in the pot see Aeschylus, fragment 122 in S. Radt, ed., *Tragicorum Graecorum Fragmenta*, vol. 3, *Aeschylus* (Göttingen: Vandenhoeck and Ruprecht, 1985), and Aristophanes, *Frogs*, 1190.

5. The feet piercing has never been fully explained. Vladimir Propp in "Oedipus in the Light of Folklore" (in *Oedipus: A Folklore Casebook*, ed. Edmunds and A. Dundes [New York: Garland, 1983], 93) suggests tha serves to place the marks of death on the child. The motif occasionally faces in later adaptations of the Oedipus myth—for example, in a tv century Latin version of the life of Judas Iscariot. See L. Edmunds, *O The Ancient Legend and Its Later Analogues* (Baltimore: Johns Hop) versity Press, 1985), 61. But this is probably derived from ' version.

6. See Herodotus, *Histories*, 1.112 and 5.92; also E' 954–63. See in general Robert Garland, *The Greek Way of Lif* nell University Press, 1990), 84. The baby's arousal of pity executioners reappears, doubtless independently, in the *R* see Léopolde Constans, *La Légende d'Oedipe* (Paris, 1881 Reprints, 1974), 172–73.

7. Garland, *Greek Way of Life*, 86.

8. The dramatists are (in addition to Euripide' Philocles, Theodectes, and Xenocles. Versions of the attested to by such later writers as Diogenes the C uncertain figure of Nicomachus. See Augustus Na' *rum Graecorum Fragmenta*, 2d ed., ed. A. Nauck/

9. This and the following passage are 1182–95. The translation, which I have slig) Lattimore in *Aristophanes, Four Comedies* Arbor: University of Michigan Press, 1969),

10. See Herodotus, *Histories*, 1.112-'

11. See Jean-Marc Moret, *Oedipe* Institut Suisse de Rome, 1984), vol. 1 Bremmer, "Oedipus and the Greek (*Greek Mythology*, ed. J. Bremmer (L/

12. This form of the riddle is ' two of the Byzantine manuscrip' Euripides' *Phoenician Women* (F Athenaeus of Naucratis, *Profe* century A.D.), 10.456b, *(Tragodoumena)*, by the his' the middle of the fourth c the riddle goes back to at

27. Jean-Pierre Vernant, "Ambiguity and Reversal: On the Enigmatic Structure of *Oedipus Rex*," in Jean-Pierre Vernant and Pierre Vidal-Naquet, *Myth and Tragedy in Ancient Greece* (Atlantic Highlands, N.J.: Humanities Press, 1981), 87–119; hereafter cited in text. See also his later discussion, "From Oedipus to Periander: Lameness, Tyranny, Incest in Legend and History," *Arethusa* 15 (1982): 19–38, which views the myth in terms of the contradictions and tensions surrounding the archaic and classical views of the tyrant.

28. René Girard, *Violence and the Sacred*, trans. P. Gregory (Baltimore: Johns Hopkins University Press, 1979), esp. 68–88; hereafter cited in text.

29. These legends may be found in Edmunds, *Oedipus: Ancient Legend*, 61–93, 144–48, 155–60 (compare the parallel story of Saint Andrew of Crete, 186–97). See also Propp, "Oedipus in the Light of Folklore," 114–18.

30. See Froma I. Zeitlin, "Thebes: Theater of Self and Society in Athenian Drama," in *Nothing to Do with Dionysus?*, 130–67, esp. 144–50.

6. Oedipus and the Trials of the Hero

1. See Propp, "Oedipus in the Light of Folklore," 109.

2. See Moret, *Oedipe, la Sphinx et les Thébains*, vol. 1, pp. 81–90, and vol. 2, plates 62 and 63.

7. Life's Tragic Shape: Plot, Design, and Destiny

1. Philip Vellacott, *Sophocles and Oedipus* (Ann Arbor: University of Michigan Press, 1971), 108.

2. Karl Reinhardt, *Sophocles*, trans. H. and D. Harvey (Oxford: Basil Blackwell, 1979), 98.

3. The Herdsman's lie is rather unusual because when Sophocles lets his character lie, he generally provides some hint in their manner of speech or some warning to the audience that a lie is being told. Presumably in this case he could assume that the story was so familiar that the audience would know the truth and realize the falsehood of the Herdsman's statement. The reference to his "fear," as well as his frightened request of Jocasta, of which we are told later (758–64), also helps us to recognize that he must be lying.

4. One may also add that Teiresias's divine knowledge was of no help in preventing the incestuous union between Oedipus and Jocasta. Presumably he might have uttered a warning at that point. Again, the conventions of the form do not permit this kind of speculation on events "outside the drama."

5. Gorgias, fragment 82 B23, in *Die Fragmente der Vorsokratiker*, 6th ed., vol. 2, ed. H. Diels and W. Kranz (Berlin: Weidmann, 1952), 305–6. The fragment is quoted by Plutarch, *On the Glory of the Athenians*, chap. 5, 348C.

6. For some suggestive remarks on the differences between time and life patterns in epic and tragedy see Bennett Simon, *The Family in Tragedy* (New Haven: Yale University Press, 1988), 13–21, 59–60.

7. See Peter Brooks, "Freud's Masterplot: A Model for Narrative," in his *Reading for the Plot* (New York: Vintage Books, 1985), 90–112, esp. 101–9.

8. François Marie Arouet de Voltaire, *Lettres sur Oedipe*, letter 3, in *Oeuvres Complètes de Voltaire*, vol. 2, ed. Louis Moland (Paris: Garnier Frères, 1877), 18–28.

9. See my *Dionysiac Poetics and Euripides' Bacchae* (Princeton: Princeton University Press, 1982), 42–45.

8. The Crisis of the City and the King

1. How many figures were actually onstage in this opening scene is a matter of controversy, but it seems likely that Sophocles would have had enough extras to simulate an actual supplication scene. For discussion and bibliography see Peter Burian, "The Play Before the Prologue: Initial Tableaux on the Greek Stage," in *Ancient and Modern: Essays in Honor of Gerald F. Else*, ed. John H. D'Arms and John W. Eadie (Ann Arbor: University of Michigan Press, 1977), 79–94, esp. 83 and 91–94.

2. Seneca's *Oedipus* has Creon mention the crossroads early in the play (line 278), but Oedipus takes no notice of the word. His recognition is to come through the ghost of Laius, not through his own investigative energy.

3. This interpretation requires a widely accepted emendation of the Greek text at line 293: "doer" for the manuscripts' "seer."

4. This is the solution adopted by Fagles in his stage direction after lines 446 and 456. This follows the interpretation of Bernard Knox, as outlined in "Sophocles, *Oedipus Tyrannos* 446: Exit Oedipus?" *Greek, Roman and Byzantine Studies* 21 (1980): 321–32, and his *Essays Ancient and Modern* (Baltimore: Johns Hopkins University Press, 1989), 146–47. See my review of the latter in *Arion* (3d ser.) 1, no. 1 (1990): 221.

5. Compare with Oedipus's phrase, "blood of the same race" (1406), in his self-accusation after the discovery.

9. Discovery and Reversal

1. The word for "all" in Oedipus's phrase, "I killed them all," is an emphatic collective form, *sympantes*, meaning "all together"—a less common word than the simple term for all, *pantes*. We have heard this word just some 60 lines before, when Jocasta gave her account of this event: "There were five in all" (*sympantes*, 752).

2. Jean Cocteau will develop this aspect of Jocasta with a characteristically modern psychology in *The Infernal Machine*.

3. R. D. Dawe, ed., *Sophocles: Oedipus Rex* (Cambridge: Cambridge University Press, 1982), 190 (on ll. 922–23).

4. The ironies of Oedipus's ignorance are reflected in a number of plays on the name Oedipus that are not easily translated into English: for instance, *ouk eidôs*, "not knowing" (1008), and *ouk oid'; ho dous*, "I do not know; the man who gave [the child]" (1038).

5. *Oid(a)*, "I know" (1038), is, of course, first person, and there is a strong syntactical pause after it; nevertheless, the pun would be heard by an audience sensitized to the ubiquitous plays on Oedipus's name.

6. Dawe, *Sophocles: Oedipus Rex*, 214 (commentary on l. 1175).

7. The translation of the last clause (1222) is not entirely certain, and commentators are divided. The sequence of particles seems to me to favor the translation I have given in the text, and Dawe prefers the same meaning in his commentary. Fagles translates it, "And now you bring down night upon my eyes," following R. C. Jebb, *Sophocles: The Plays and Fragments*, pt. 1, *The Oedipus Tyrannus*, 3d ed. (Cambridge: Cambridge University Press, 1893), 161.

10. Resolution: Tragic Suffering, Heroic Endurance

1. See George Devereux, "The Self-Blinding of Oidipous in Sophokles: *Oidipous Tyrannos*," *Journal of Hellenic Studies* 93 (1973): 36–49.

2. In his famous Funeral Speech, delivered a few years at the most before *Oedipus Tyrannus* was performed, Pericles commended the common Athenian view that the women of Athens should be as inconspicuous among men as possible, whether for praise or blame (Thucydides, *The Peloponnesian War*, 2.45.2).

3. See especially lines 924–26 and Bernard Knox's comment in *Oedipus at Thebes*, 183–84.

4. Fagles's translation of line 1334 ("What good were eyes to me?") is a beautiful touch, suggesting (intentionally?) Shakespeare's Gloucester in *King Lear* 4.1.18: "I have no way, and therefore want no eyes."

5. In *Ajax*, an earlier Sophoclean play, the hero's final address to the light is the prelude to his suicide (*Ajax*, 856–58). In *Ajax* (658ff) and in *Antigone* (1232ff) possession of a sword is the prelude to suicide. Thus Sophocles may have been deliberately arousing an expectation in *Oedipus Tyrannus*, only to surprise us later by not fulfilling it.

6. It is interesting to compare this with Herodotus's tale of the accidental killing of Croesus's son by Adrastus, which has a number of parallels with *Oedipus Tyrannus*, especially the motif of trying to evade an oracle that is tragically fulfilled after all. The unfortunate Adrastus, who is not legally guilty of homicide, does in fact commit suicide (*Histories*, 1.45).

7. In line 1325 Oedipus addresses the chorus, "You do not escape my knowledge, but I know you clearly." Richard Jebb, commenting on this verse

in his *Oedipus Tyrannus,* suggests that there is "a distinct echo" here of the *Iliad* 24.563, Achilles' speech to King Priam as the former is about to ransom Hector's body: "I recognize you, Priam, in my heart, nor are you hidden from me." The Homeric resonance of this magnanimity between a Greek chief and his helpless suppliant gives Oedipus's lines here an atmosphere of epic grandeur and heroism. By having Oedipus speak Achilles' lines, however, Sophocles reverses the Homeric relation between the strong (Achilles) and the weak (Priam), and thus perhaps suggests the new inner strength emerging in Oedipus.

8. Pope Gregory does this in the medieval and Christian version of his Oedipus-like life.

9. See J. C. Kamerbeek, *The Plays of Sophocles,* pt. 4, *The Oedipus Tyrannus* (Leiden: Brill, 1967), 256, on lines 1411–12.

10. A performance of the play at the Odéon Theater in Paris in the summer of 1985, for example, staged the last scene with a naked Oedipus, splashed with blood, standing before his daughters.

11. See Bernard Knox, *The Heroic Temper* (Berkeley and Los Angeles: University of California Press, 1964), chap. 1, esp. pp. 7ff.

11. Inner Vision and Theatrical Spectacle

1. For a discussion of the "other scene" (*anderer Schauplatz*), see Lacan, *Ecrits,* 193, 264, 284f.

2. This translation attempts to bring out the force of the repetition *tiktousan . . . dusteknon* (1247f); the repeated root *tek-* ("give birth to") hammers home the horror of the doubled "mothering." Note the triple repetition of the root *tek-* in line 1250.

3. On the symbolic reenactment of the union—although with a very different interpretation—see John Hay, *Lame Knowledge and the Homosporic Womb* (Washington, D.C.: University of America Press, 1978) 103ff and 133f.

4. See also the Messenger's earlier description (l. 1262) of Oedipus's bursting through the "enclosures" (the doors) to Jocasta's chamber. The repetition of the same word in all three of these passages (*klêithra*) emphasizes the opening up of an enclosed, invisible space to theatrical vision.

5. Propp, "Oedipus in the Light of Folklore," 76–121, esp. 113–14.

6. Translation by Michael Jameson in *Complete Greek Tragedies,* ed. David Grene and Richmond Lattimore, vol. 2, *Sophocles* (Chicago: University of Chicago Press, 1959), 312.

7. John Jones, *On Aristotle and Greek Tragedy* (London: Chatto & Windus, 1962), esp. 24ff, 35ff, and 41ff (on *Poetics,* 6, 1450a2f).

8. This self-consciousness about drama's special mode of revealing the self through narration of what is hidden in interior space may owe something to the transitional moment of tragedy between an oral and a literate culture. See my *Interpreting Greek Tragedy: Myth, Poetry, Text,* 75–109.

Selected Bibliography

PRIMARY WORKS

Editions and Commentaries

Dawe, R.D. *Sophocles: Oedipus Tyrannus*. Cambridge: Cambridge University Press, 1982.

Gould, Thomas. *Oedipus the King, by Sophocles*. Englewood Cliffs, N.J.: Prentice-Hall, 1970. Prose translation and running commentary with a heavily Freudian slant.

Jebb, Richard C. *Sophocles: The Plays and Fragments: Part 1, The Oedipus Tyrannus*. 3d ed. Cambridge: Cambridge University Press, 1893. Extensive introduction, Greek text, facing translation in fairly literal prose, and commentary. Still the most usable all-around edition of the play.

Lloyd-Jones, Hugh, and N. G. Wilson. *Sophoclis Fabulae*. Oxford Classical Texts. Oxford: Clarendon Press, 1990. The standard Greek text of Sophocles.

Sheppard, John T. *The Oedipus Tyrannus of Sophocles*. Cambridge: Cambridge University Press, 1920. Greek text, facing translation, interpretative essays emphasizing the moral innocence of Oedipus, and commentary.

Translations

Bagg, Robert. *Sophocles: Oedipus Tyrannus*. Amherst: University of Massachusetts Press, 1982. A brisk and spirited contemporary verse translation.

Berg, Stephen, and Diskin Clay. *Sophocles: Oedipus the King*. New York: Oxford University Press, 1978. Collaboration of a poet and a classicist; an imaginative effort to catch the poetic flavor of Sophocles' language. Brief, helpful introduction. Highly recommended.

167

Cook, Albert, and Edwin Dolin. *An Anthology of Greek Tragedy*. Indianapolis: Bobbs-Merrill, 1972. Contains fairly literal translations of *Oedipus Tyrannus* and *Oedipus at Colonus*; helpful introduction and bibliographies.

Fagles, Robert. *Sophocles: The Three Theban Plays*, Harmondsworth and New York: Penguin Classics, 1984. Combines clarity with the poetic quality and emotional energy of the play; slightly expands the original. Excellent introductory essays by Bernard Knox. Highly recommended.

Fitts, Dudley, and Robert Fitzgerald. *The Oedipus Cycle*, New York: Harcourt, Brace & World, 1948. Elegant and readable verse translation, but freer than Grene, Fagles, or Berg and Clay, especially in the choral odes.

Grene, David. *Oedipus the King* and *Oedipus at Colonus*. In *The Complete Greek Tragedies*, vol. 2, edited by David Grene and Richmond Lattimore. Chicago: University of Chicago Press, 1959. Serviceable freeverse translation, close to the Greek, but sometimes prosaic. Also available in Phoenix Paperbacks and Modern Library editions.

Knox, Bernard M. W. *Sophocles: Oedipus the King*. New York: Washington Square Press, 1959. Straightforward prose version intended for acting.

Watling, E. F. *Sophocles: The Theban Plays*. Harmondsworth and New York: Penguin Classics, 1947. Lucid and readable but dry; follows Sophocles' imagery rather less closely than Grene or Fagles.

Yeats, William Butler. *The Collected Plays*. London: Macmillan, 1953. Contains versions of *Oedipus Tyrannus* and *Oedipus at Colonus*; rhythmic prose intended for the stage. The choruses have many beautiful touches but are much abridged.

Related Primary Texts

Aeschylus. *Seven against Thebes*. In *The Complete Greek Tragedies*, vol. 1, edited by David Grene and Richmond Lattimore. Chicago: University of Chicago Press, 1959.

Aristotle. *Poetics*. In *Ancient Literary Criticism*, translated and edited by David Russell and Michael Winterbottom. Oxford: Oxford University Press, 1972.

Euripides. *Hippolytus, Ion, Phoenician Women*. In *The Complete Greek Tragedies, Euripides*, vols. 3 and 4, edited by David Grene and Richmond Lattimore. Chicago: University of Chicago Press, 1959.

Herodotus. *The Persian Wars*. Translated by George Rawlinson. New York: Modern Library, 1942.

Homer. *The Odyssey*. Translated by Richmond Lattimore. New York: Harper & Row, 1965.

Seneca. *Oedipus*. In *Seneca, Four Tragedies and Octavia*, translated by E. F. Watling. Harmondsworth and New York: Penguin Classics, 1966.

Thucydides. *The Peloponnesian War.* Translated by Rex Warner. Harmondsworth and New York: Penguin Classics, 1954.

Anthologies

Berkowitz, Luci, and Theodore F. Brunner, eds. *Oedipus Tyrannus.* New York: Norton, 1970. Contains prose translation of *Oedipus Tyrannus,* selections from the *Odyssey,* Thucydides on the plague, Euripides' *Phoenician Women,* and selected anthropological and literary criticism.

Cook, Albert, ed. *Oedipus Rex: A Mirror for Greek Drama.* Belmont, Calif.: Wadsworth, 1963; reprint, Prospect Heights, Ill.: Waveland Press, 1982. Contains translations of *Oedipus Tyrannus* and *Poetics* and critical statements and essays from Voltaire to the present.

Kallich, Michael, Andrew MacLeish, and Gertrude Schoenbohm, eds. *Oedipus Myth and Drama.* New York: Odyssey Press, 1968. Contains a modernized version of Jebb's translation of *Oedipus Tyrannus,* Aristotle's *Poetics,* the Oedipus plays of Dryden and Lee and Hofmannsthal, and selected literary, anthropological, and psychoanalytic criticism.

Sanderson, James L., and Everett Zimmerman, *Oedipus: Myth and Dramatic Form.* Boston: Houghton Mifflin, 1968. Contains Watling's translation of *Oedipus Tyrannus;* the *Oedipus* of Seneca, Voltaire, and Gide; Cocteau's *Infernal Machine* (all in translation); and selections from Aristotle, Freud, and modern critics.

SECONDARY WORKS

Bibliographies

Buxton, R. G. A. *Sophocles, Greece and Rome.* Supplement. *New Surveys in the Classics,* no. 16. Oxford: Clarendon Press, 1984.

Johansen, H. Friis. "Sophocles 1939–1959." *Lustrum* 7 (1962): 94–342.

Saïd, Suzanne. "Bibliographie tragique, 1900–88." *Métis* 3 (1988): 409–512, esp. 468–84.

Historical, Cultural, and Archeological Background

Baldry, H. C. *The Greek Tragic Theater.* London: Chatto & Windus, 1971. Useful brief discussion of the Greek theater in its social and historical context.

Bieber, Margarete. *The History of the Greek and Roman Theater.* 2d ed. Princeton: Princeton University Press, 1961. Well-illustrated presentation of the archeological evidence for Greek dramatic performances.

Bowra, C. M. *The Greek Experience.* Cleveland: World, 1957. Attempts to define the character of early Greek civilization by surveying its major cultural achievements.

Burn, A. R. *Pericles and Athens*. New York: Collier, 1962. Readable account of the rise and fall of Periclean Athens.

Easterling, P. E., and B. M. W. Knox, eds. *Cambridge History of Classical Literature*. Vol. 1. Cambridge: Cambridge University Press, 1985. Standard history of Greek literature, with chapters on the tragedians and dramatic festivals, chronologies, and useful bibliographies.

Guthrie, W. K. C. *A History of Greek Philosophy*. Vols. 2 and 3. Cambridge: Cambridge University Press, 1965, 1969. Detailed account of Greek thought in the age of the tragedians.

Hammond, N. G. L. *A History of Greece to 322* B.C. 2d ed. Oxford: Clarendon Press, 1967. A standard history of Greece.

Kirk, Geoffrey S.; J. E. Raven; and M. Scholfield. *The Presocratic Philosophers*. 2d ed. Cambridge: Cambridge University Press, 1983. Texts, translations, commentaries on thinkers contemporary with *Oedipus Tyrannus*.

Pickard-Cambridge, Arthur W. *Dithyramb, Tragedy and Comedy*. 2d ed. Revised by T. B. L. Webster. Oxford: Oxford University Press, 1962.

——. *The Dramatic Festivals of Athens*. 2d ed. Revised by John Gould and D. M. Lewis. Oxford: Oxford University Press, 1968.

——. *The Theater of Dionysus at Athens*. Oxford: Oxford University Press, 1946. Pickard-Cambridge's three books are still the fullest documentation for the origin, nature, and physical arrangements of the dramatic festivals. Not for beginners.

Rodenwaldt, Gerhart, and Walter Hege. *The Acropolis*. 2d ed. Oxford: Basil Blackwell, 1957. Brief descriptive account of the major monuments on the Acropolis and Pericles' building program; excellent photographs.

Criticism: Books and Parts of Books

Ahl, Frederick. *Sophocles' Oedipus: Evidence and Self-Conviction*. Ithaca: Cornell University Press, 1991. A radical rereading, arguing that Oedipus is mistaken in accepting the evidence that he is Jocasta's son and Laius's killer. Many stimulating and acute observations, but ultimately unconvincing.

Bloom, Harold, ed. *Sophocles' Oedipus Rex*. New York: Chelsea House Publishers, 1988. Selected recent criticism.

Bowra, C. M. *Sophoclean Tragedy*. Oxford: Oxford University Press, 1944. Focuses on moral and legal issues in the play, with a rather moralistic view.

Cameron, Alister. *The Identity of Oedipus the King*. New York: New York University Press, 1965. Somewhat rambling essays, emphasizing theme of self-discovery.

Eden, Kathy. *Poetic and Legal Fiction in the Aristotelian Tradition.* Princeton: Princeton University Press, 1986. On the importance of rhetoric, law courts, and legal proof and argument in the ancient view of tragedy.

Edmunds, Lowell, ed. *Oedipus: The Ancient Legend and Its Later Analogues.* Baltimore: Johns Hopkins University Press, 1984. Companion volume to Edmunds and Dundes, below. Comparative material for history and diffusion of Oedipus myth.

Edmunds, Lowell, and Alan Dundes. *Oedipus: A Folklore Casebook.* New York: Garland, 1983.

Ehrenberg, Victor. *Sophocles and Pericles.* Oxford: Blackwell, 1954. Studies *Oedipus Tyrannus* and *Angigone* in terms of the political currents of the time.

Else, Gerald F. *Aristotle's Poetics: The Argument.* Cambridge: Harvard University Press, 1967. New translation and detailed analysis of crucial sections of *Poetics*, with a fundamental reexamination of the "tragic flaw" theory.

Euben, J. Peter, ed. *Greek Tragedy and Political Theory.* Berkeley and Los Angeles: University of California Press, 1986. Essays on the relation of tragedy to social and political thought.

Freud, Sigmund. *The Interpretation of Dreams.* 3d ed. Translated and edited by James Strachey. New York: Basic Books, 1955. Contains what is perhaps the most influential view of *Oedipus Tyrannus* in the twentieth century.

Gellie, George. *Sophocles: A Reading.* Melbourne: University of Melbourne Press, 1972. Good study of the dramatic movement of *Oedipus Tyrannus*; helpful general essays on plot, character, gods, poetry in Sophocles as a whole.

Gentili, Bruno, and A. Pretagostini, eds. *Edipo: Il teatro greco e la cultura Europea.* Rome: Edizioni del Ateneo, 1986. Multilingual publication of an international conference on Oedipus; essays on many aspects of the play, myth, later influences.

Girard, René. *The Violence and the Sacred.* Translated by P. Gregory. Baltimore: Johns Hopkins University Press, 1979.

Goldhill, Simon. *Reading Greek Tragedy.* Cambridge: Cambridge University Press, 1986. Stimulating contemporary criticism of a wide range of Greek plays, including a chapter on *Oedipus Tyrannus*.

Jones, John. *On Aristotle and Greek Tragedy.* London: Chatto & Windus, 1962. Emphasizes the importance of plot and action rather than the depiction of character in Greek tragedy.

Kirkwood, G. M. *A Study of Sophoclean Drama.* Ithaca: Cornell University Press, 1958. A clear topic-by-topic study of formal elements and dramatic structure in the seven plays.

Kitto, H. D. F. *Poiesis: Structure and Thought.* Berkeley and Los Angeles: University of California Press, 1966. Contains a detailed discussion of *Oedipus Tyrannus.*

_____. *Sophocles: Dramatist and Philosopher.* London: Oxford University Press, 1958.

Knox, Bernard M. W. *Oedipus at Thebes.* New Haven: Yale University Press, 1957. A careful study of Sophocles' language and imagery, suggesting that Oedipus is a distillation of Athens in its greatness, power, and danger.

_____. *The Heroic Temper: Studies in Sophoclean Tragedy.* Berkeley and Los Angeles: University of California Press, 1964. On the darker side of the Sophoclean hero.

_____. *Word and Action: Essays on the Ancient Theatre.* Baltimore and London: Johns Hopkins University Press, 1979. Contains several important essays on the historical circumstances of *Oedipus Tyrannus.*

Lattimore, Richmond. *The Poetry of Greek Tragedy.* Baltimore: Johns Hopkins University Press, 1958. Excellent discussion of the foundling theme in *Oedipus Tyrannus.*

Letters, F. J. H. *The Life and Work of Sophocles.* London: Sheed and Ward, 1953. Useful discussion of cultural background, life, personality of Sophocles; sensible criticism of the moralistic view of *Oedipus Tyrannus.*

Mueller, Martin. *The Children of Oedipus.* Toronto: University of Toronto Press, 1980. Studies modern imitations of Greek tragedy from 1550 to 1800, with a valuable chapter on *Oedipus Tyrannus.*

O'Brien, Michael J. *Twentieth Century Interpretations of Oedipus Rex.* Englewood Cliffs, N.J.: Prentice-Hall, 1968. A good selection of critical essays and brief comments about *Oedipus Tyrannus.*

Poole, Adrian. *Tragedy: Shakespeare and the Greek Example.* Oxford: Blackwell, 1986. Attempts to define the qualities of the Greek tragic view by juxtaposing readings of Greek drama, including *Oedipus Tyrannus,* and Shakespeare.

Pucci, Pietro. *Oedipus and the Fabrication of the Father.* Baltimore: Johns Hopkins University Press, 1992. A poststructuralist approach, emphasizing the connections between the riddles, language, paternity, and textuality.

Reinhardt, Karl. *Sophocles.* Translated by H. and D. Harvey. Oxford: Basil Blackwell, 1979. Full of insights into philosophical and formal aspects of play; stresses the evolution of Sophocles' drama from play to play and the centrality of illusion and reality in *Oedipus Tyrannus.* Highly recommended.

Rudnytsky, Peter L. *Freud and Oedipus.* New York: Columbia University Press, 1987. A detailed study of the psychoanalytic approach to the Oedipus myth.

Scodel, Ruth. *Sophocles.* Boston: Twayne Publishers, 1984. An introduction to all of Sophocles for the general reader.

Seale, David. *Vision and Stagecraft in Sophocles.* Chicago: University of Chicago Press, 1982. Chapter on *Oedipus Tyrannus* traces the theme of sight, blindness, eyes, and other visual phenomena.

Segal, Charles. *Interpreting Greek Tragedy.* Ithaca: Cornell University Press, 1986. Uses a variety of contemporary critical approaches to Greek drama and offers a number of different perspectives on *Oedipus Tyrannus.*

____. "Sophocles." In *Ancient Writers: Greece and Rome,* vol. 1, edited by T. J. Luce, 179–207. New York: Scribners, 1982. A brief overview of Sophocles' life, times, and dramatic art.

____. *Tragedy and Civilization: An Interpretation of Sophocles.* Cambridge: Harvard University Press, 1981. A study of Sophocles against the background of myth, views of nature, man, and society. Contains detailed chapters on *Oedipus Tyrannus* and *Oedipus at Colonus.*

Segal, Erich. *Oxford Readings in Greek Tragedy.* Oxford: Oxford University Press, 1983. Useful collection of authoritative recent criticism. Includes E. R. Dodds, "On Misinterpreting the *Oedipus Rex.*"

Steiner, George. *Antigones.* Oxford: Oxford University Press, 1984. A detailed, sensitive study of literary variations on *Antigone,* with many points of contact with *Oedipus Tyrannus.*

Vernant, Jean-Pierre, and Pierre Vidal-Naquet. *Tragedy and Myth in Ancient Greece.* Translated by Janet Lloyd. Atlantic Highlands, N.J.: Humanities Press, 1981. Contains two valuable essays on *Oedipus Tyrannus.*

____. *Myth and Tragedy in Ancient Greece.* Translated by Janet Lloyd. New York: Zone Books, 1988. More complete collection of Vernant and Vidal-Naquet's essays on tragedy.

Vickers, Brian. *Towards Greek Tragedy.* London: Longmans, 1979. Large-scale study of Greek tragedy, emphasizing the connections between myth, drama, and ritual from an anthropological perspective.

Waldock, A. J. A. *Sophocles the Dramatist.* Cambridge: Cambridge University Press, 1951. Brilliantly but narrowly argues that Sophocles' chief concern is dramatic effect, even at the expense of coherence of plot or meaning. Useful cautionary remarks on the "documentary fallacy," although the author falls into his own "theatrical fallacy."

Webster, T. B. L. *An Introduction to Sophocles.* Oxford: Oxford University Press, 1936. Well-focused, detailed discussions of Sophocles' life, thought, characterization, plot, odes.

Whitman, Cedric H. *Sophocles: A Study of Heroic Humanism.* Cambridge: Harvard University Press, 1951. Elegant refutation of the "tragic flaw" approach to *Oedipus Tyrannus*; views the play as a tragedy of irrational suffering.

Winnington-Ingram, R. P. *Sophocles: An Interpretation.* Cambridge: Cambridge University Press, 1980. Especially helpful on the religious background of *Oedipus Tyrannus* and its roots in archaic thought.

Woodard, Thomas. *Sophocles: A Collection of Critical Essays.* Englewood Cliffs, N.J.: Prentice-Hall, 1966.

Articles

Buxton, R. G. A. "Blindness and Its Limits: Sophocles and the Logic of Myth." *Journal of Hellenic Studies* 100 (1980): 22–37.

de Kock, E. L. "The Sophoklean Oidipous and Its Antecedents." *Acta Classica* 4 (1961): 7–28.

Dodds, E. R. "On Misunderstanding the *Oedipus Rex.*" *Greece and Rome* 13 (1966): 37–49. Included in anthologies of O'Brien and E. Segal.

Edmunds, Lowell. "The Cults and the Legend of Oedipus." *Harvard Studies in Classical Philology* 85 (1981): 221–38.

____. "Oedipus in the Middle Ages." *Antike und Abendland* 25 (1976): 140–55.

Goodhart, Sandor. "*Leistas Ephaske*: Oedipus and Laius' Many Murderers." *Diacritics* 8, no. 1 (1978): 55–71.

Gould, Thomas. "The Innocence of Oedipus: The Philosophers on *Oedipus the King.*" *Arion* 4 (1965): 363–86, 582–611; *Arion* 5 (1966): 478–525.

Musurillo, Herbert. "Sunken Imagery in Sophocles' *Oedipus.*" *American Journal of Philology* 78 (1957): 36–51.

Newton, Rick M. "*Hippolytus* and the Dating of *Oedipus Tyrannus.*" *Greek, Roman and Byzantine Studies* 21 (1980): 5–22.

Segal, Charles. "Sacral Kingship and Tragic Heroism in Five Oedipus Plays and *Hamlet.*" *Helios* 5 (1977): 1–10.

____. "Synaesthesia in Sophocles." *Illinois Classical Studies* 2 (1977): 86–96.

Smith, Susan Harris. "Twentieth-Century Plays Using Classical Mythic Themes: A Checklist." *Modern Drama* 29 (1986): 110–33, esp. 124–25.

Vernant, Jean-Pierre. "From Oedipus to Periander: Lameness, Tyranny, Incest in Legend and History." *Arethusa* 15 (1982): 19–38. Reprinted in 1988 collection of Vernant and Vidal-Naquet.

Index

Index

plot, 155; in *Oedipus Tyrannus*,
83–86
plowing, metaphor of, 86, 133,
135–36. *See also* agriculture;
seed; sowing
Plutarch, *Consolation to
Apollonius*, 82
Poetics, by Aristotle, 12, 16,
19–20, 40, 76, 121, 155
pollution: metaphor of, 20, 40,
47, 80–81, 90, 97, 99, 103,
105, 127, 136, 141–44,
146–47; in Seneca, 21; Jean-
Pierre Vernant on, 65; *See
also* plague; purification
Polybus, 62, 115, 125, 128, 141;
death of, 122–23, 131, 133
Polyclitus, 7
Polygnotus, 4
Polyneices, 18, 45, 55,
Potniae, 48
Priam, 73, 165n7
primal scene, 148
prizes, for tragedies, 36
prologue, of *Oedipus Tyrannus*,
97–102
prophecy, 71, 75, 79, 89, 106,
107, 124. *See also* Apollo;
Delphi; oracle
Propp, Vladimir, 58, 154
Propylaea, 4
Protagoras, the sophist, 5–6
Protagoras, dialogue by Plato, 5
psychoanalysis, 14; and *Oedipus
Tyrannus*, 59–63. *See also*
Freud, Sigmund
Purcell, Henry, 29
purification, 81, 100, 134. *See
also* pollution
Pynchon, Thomas, *The Crying of
Lot 49*, 33

Racine, Jean, 38

rationalism, 5–6, 8, 91. *See also*
Enlightenment
recognition, 20, 121, 134, 154; in
Seneca, 21
Reinhardt, Karl, 77
Renaissance, *Oedipus Tyrannus*
in, 18–19
reversal, 20, 121, 125, 135, 141,
144
riddle, 52–56, 74, 86–89, 106,
108, 161n12. *See also*
Sphinx
ritual, 39, 97–99, 102, 122
Robbe-Grillet, Alain, *The Erasers*,
33
robbers, and the killing of Laius,
62, 92, 101, 113, 115, 123
Roman de Thèbes, 18
Romanticism, and *Oedipus
Tyrannus*, 25–26
Romulus and Remus, 70
Rose, H. J., 58
Rossini, Gioacchino, 29
Rukeyser, Muriel, "Myth," 33

Sachs, Hans, 18
Salamis, 3
Santayana, George, 93
satyr play, 36, 46
scapegoat, 22, 65, 66, 94, 141
Schiller, Friedrich von, *Bride of
Messina*, 25
Schopenhauer, Arthur, 26
Schubert, Franz, 29
sea, metaphor of, 99, 103, 122,
133
seeds, metaphor of, 62, 104, 149.
See also agriculture,
plowing, sowing
self, in Greek tragedy, 155–56
self-blinding, 24, 40, 45–47, 51,
72–73, 81, 83, 101, 134–39,

181

The Author

Charles Segal received his A.B. (1957) and Ph.D. (1961) from Harvard University, where he is currently professor of Greek and Latin. He has taught at the University of Pennsylvania and at Brown and Princeton universities and has held a Fulbright fellowship at the American School of Classical Studies in Athens and a Prix de Rome at the American Academy, where he served as Resident Scholar in Classics in 1986. A senior fellow at the Center for Hellenic Studies in Washington, D.C. (1987–92), Professor Segal has been awarded fellowships from the Center for Hellenic Studies, the American Council of Learned Societies, the Guggenheim Foundation, the National Endowment for the Humanities, and the Center for Advanced Study in Behavioral Sciences. He is a fellow of the American Academy of Arts and Sciences and is president-elect of the American Philological Association.

His books include *Tragedy and Civilization: An Interpretation of Sophocles* (1981), *Dionysiac Poetics and Euripides' "Bacchae"* (1982), *Interpreting Greek Tragedy* (1986), *Pindar's Mythmaking* (1986), *Language and Desire in Seneca's "Phaedra"* (1986), *La musique du Sphinx* (1987), *Orpheus: The Myth of the Poet* (1989), and *Lucretius on Death and Anxiety* (1990).

DATE			

257
H

HARDON, J.

ALL MY LIBERTY

DATE DUE	BORROWER'S NAME	ROOM NUMBER